Did You Know?

BOOK 2

By

Dr. Keith A. Rothra

About the Author

Dr. Keith Rothra is Senior Pastor of Judson Community Baptist Church in Longview, Texas. Through thirty years in ministry, he has served in churches in Alabama, Virginia, Arkansas, Illinois, and Texas. He has served as Youth Minister, Worship Leader, Associate Pastor, Interim Pastor, and Senior Pastor in various congregations.

Raised in Celoron, New York, he graduated from Arizona State University, Troy University, and Covington Theological Seminary.

After seven years in the US Navy, he returned to college and then entered the US Air Force. He served as a combat aircrew member in C-130 aircraft for nine years, and then nine years as a war planner before retiring as a Major.

Married to Barbara for over forty years, they have two children and six grandchildren. Keith enjoys playing his guitar, singing his gospel music creations, and sharing his hundreds of short devotional writings, some of which are found in this book.

ISBN-13: 978-1535055581
ISBN-10: 1535055588

Contents

6

Introduction

A mid-night experience with my dear bride, Barbara, was the beginning of DID YOU KNOW?. She has a way of asking me questions at dark-thirty at night. She nudged me in the back about six times before I was awake enough to understand that she was about to unload a new midnight nugget. Actually, it was well past midnight … closer to 3:00 AM.

She had been reading her Bible. She's a night person and does a lot of her scripture reading at dark hours. But when she has a question, she takes the scriptures quite literally where Paul told the women to ask their husbands at home. The 3:00 AM hour has never been a deterrent to her. I asked her once if these discussions could wait for morning, and she replied that she could always call her Pastor. Even at 3:00 AM, I knew she would have no problem with picking up her cell phone and calling me with her question just to get her Pastor's response.

Here is her beginning question: Did you know, in the New Jerusalem there will be one continuous day; never a night? But there will be a river flowing through the city, and it will have fruit trees on both sides of the river. The fruit will have a new crop every month. So … are you ready for this at 3:00 AM? …. If there is no night, only one continuous day .. how long is a month?

This and similar questions became the stimulus for me to answer the questions in a short format.   Then, it graduated into reading short scripture passages and commenting on them in about 400 words.   Then I began posting them as a daily blog on Facebook.

When I passed the 100-mark on Did You Know dailies, I realized that God was giving me a book to share.   This is the second volume of Did You Know.   I have begun formatting volumes three and four for future publication.

What began with a middle-of-the-night question from my dear wife, Barbara, and began with the words, "Did you know?," has grown to at least four volumes of inspirations.

Our prayers are that you will draw encouragement from what the Lord has given us to share, and that you will share it with others.

Dr. Keith A. Rothra, Pastor
Judson Community Baptist Church
2 Timothy 2:2

Acknowledgements

To attempt to share what is within these pages without the Divine inspiration of our Holy Father would not only be foolhardy, but, I believe, impossible.   The daily nudge from my Lord compelled me to write yet another contribution each day for a year and a half.   There were times when I would crawl into bed at night and begin to set the alarm for the morning, when I would be reminded that I couldn't sleep until I opened the Bible and poured out another day's contribution.

Therefore, before anyone else, I must give honor and glory to my Lord, Jesus Christ, for His daily inspiration to make these writings possible.

Barbara Gibbons Rothra, my bride for nearly a half century, has encouraged me daily, and found the patience to push me forward and, once the pieces were written, to put them into a book format.

Day after day I have put these spiritual vitamin pills onto Facebook for others to share.   I thank the many Facebook "friends," and friends they certainly have been, for their "likes" and "shares" that have made me realize that Did You Know? was reaching God's people with a message that inspires.

Therefore, to my church family at Judson Community Baptist Church, my Facebook family, and my wife, children, and grandchildren, I offer my sincere gratitude.   To my Lord, I acknowledge the true inspiration and prodding that made me continue. I hope His Kingdom, and all who are part of it, will be blessed by the words found in this volume.

Dr. Keith A. Rothra, Pastor
Judson Community Baptist Church

1 GOD DOESN'T LIVE THERE

DID YOU KNOW?

King David, the psalmist, once wrote, "I was glad when they said, 'Let us go up to the House of the Lord.'" His heart rejoiced at the very idea of going to the tabernacle. He would bring sacrifices to be offered as a statement of thanks for the many gifts that God rained down upon him and all Israel. But why did they go to the tabernacle? Did the Lord of Lords live in that tabernacle? Can a tent of meeting possibly house the One who cannot be enclosed by the starry hosts of heaven?

David was not allowed to build a temple for God, but the Lord allowed his son, King Solomon, to create one in Jerusalem. Solomon went all about his great kingdom and beyond gathering the right materials for a building that might be worthy of calling it a House of God. But even Solomon knew that his temple could not contain God. He expressed it in 2 Chronicles.

> *The temple that I am building will be great, for our God is greater than any of the gods. But who is able to build a temple for Him, since even heaven and the highest heaven cannot contain Him? Who am I then that I should build a temple for Him except as a place to burn incense before Him?* ***2 Chronicles 2:5-6 (HCSB)***

Today we go to "church."   Many people think that the church is that building where everybody gathers, but the truth is that the church is not the building, but the people who gather there.   And we all know that we can pray to God at home, in our car, at the marketplace, or even at the Super Bowl.   God will hear your prayer wherever you are.   After all, like Solomon noted, God does not live there.

So why do we go to church when God doesn't live there? ...especially when He hears your prayers wherever you are? We are told in Hebrews this caution:

> *... not staying away from our [worship] meetings, as some habitually do, but encouraging each other, and all the more as you see the day drawing near.*
> **Hebrews 10:25 (HCSB)**

We should come together to worship the Lord in unity and to encourage one another to continue on the narrow path we are called to walk.   Just as a single thread has little strength and several woven together can hold much greater weight, so can a lone believer be led astray, but with the strength of others, we can resist.

The church building is not where God lives.   He lives in your heart...the real temple.   But He brings His children together to worship Him at the place we call "church."

2 BLOOD AND FROGS

DID YOU KNOW?

The Egyptians worshipped the Nile River as one of their gods.   They saw it as a giver of life; it came every spring with floods to replenish their lower Nile delta.   But they thought that blood was repulsive.   Did you remember what God did in Egypt?

> *Go to Pharaoh in the morning. When you see him walking out to the water, stand ready to meet him by the bank of the Nile. Take in your hand the staff that turned into a snake.   This is what Yahweh says: Here is how you will know that I am Yahweh. Watch. I will strike the water in the Nile with the staff in my hand, and it will turn to blood.   The fish in the Nile will die, the river will stink, and the Egyptians will be unable to drink water from it." **Exodus 7:15, 17-18 (HCSB)**

The Egyptians also worshipped frogs.   They were seen as special gods.   Do you remember what God did in Egypt with the frogs?

> *Then the LORD said to Moses, "Go in to Pharaoh and tell him: This is what Yahweh says: Let My people go, so that they may worship Me.   But if you refuse to let them go, then I will plague all your territory with frogs. The Nile will swarm with frogs; they will come up and go into your palace, into your bedroom and on your*

bed, into the houses of your officials and your people, and into your ovens and kneading bowls. The frogs will come up on you, your people, and all your officials." Exodus 8:1-4 (HCSB)

Do you see what God did?   God took the things that the Egyptians held most dearly and made them disgusting to them.   God knew that Pharaoh's heart would not listen to Him.   Pharaoh was in love with his own beliefs and would not listen to God.

Aren't we that way sometimes?   Did you know that God can change your heart about your favorite things too?   If you are like Pharaoh, and you allow those things to shut out the will of God in your life …. don't be surprised if God starts working on your "want to's."

So when your favorite things are turning into problems … just ask God what He is trying to tell you …. Or you could be like Pharaoh and harden your heart … it didn't work so well for him.

3   DENOMINATIONALISM

DID YOU KNOW?

Brothers, I was not able to speak to you as spiritual people but as people of the flesh, as babies in Christ. I gave you milk to drink, not solid food, because you were not yet ready for it. In fact, you are still not ready, **1 Corinthians 3:1-2 (HCSB)**

I am blessed to have been called to be Pastor of a Baptist congregation.   Our group is not large, but we are a Christian family who are united in the cause of Christ.   But every now and then, I create a bit of a stir when I tell our Baptist worshippers that there will be other people there (heaven) who are not Baptist.   As a matter of fact, I remind them often that there will be no Baptists in heaven … nor Methodists … nor any other denomination.   The only people in heaven are going to be Christians … followers of Christ.

Paul challenged the church at Corinth because they divided themselves between various leaders.   Some are following Apollos, some Paul, some Peter …. etc.

… because you are still fleshly. For since there is envy and strife among you, are you not fleshly and living like unbelievers? For whenever someone says, "I'm with Paul," and another, "I'm with Apollos," are

you not [unspiritual] people?   **1 Corinthians 3:3-4 (HCSB)**

During one Bible study, my wife shocked some of the ladies in her class by saying that she didn't want to be known as a Baptist, but as a Christian.   I support that wholeheartedly. There is nothing wrong with being a Baptist or Episcopal or Lutheran, so long as you do not become so parochial in your thoughts that you think your group is the only one that is Christian.

There is one Christ.   There is one Lord.   There is one salvation, which is found only in that Lord, who is Christ. There is one Holy Spirit who is sent by the One and only Holy Father to call you to accept that One Christ.   Now, did you notice that there wasn't a single denomination mentioned there?   All mainstream Christian denominations teach such doctrine.

Denominations exist because they practice different modes of worshipping Christ, and have differences in some minor areas.   By all means, worship in honor of God, but by all means, worship Him.   And maybe we can all be surprised at who God includes in His Book of Life.

4   HANNAH'S PRAYER

DID YOU KNOW?

Children are a gift from God.   Oh, I know there are times when we wonder if that is true, but the reality is that not having any children can be a painful thing to some.   The Bible gives several examples of men and women who were childless, and God heard their prayer for a child and granted their request.   One of the most famous of these was Hannah, who was barren and wept over that fact daily.   She went to the temple and asked God to give her a son for her husband.   She even promised to give him back.

> *Making a vow, she pleaded, "LORD of Hosts, if You will take notice of Your servant's affliction, remember and not forget me, and give Your servant a son, I will give him to the LORD all the days of his life, and his hair will never be cut."*   ***1 Samuel 1:11 (HCSB)***

God heard Hannah's prayer and she gave birth to Samuel, who was raised in the temple and became the Judge of Israel.   But Hannah's was not the only prayer for a child.

Abram and Sarah were childless.   They resorted to a surrogate mother to bring their first child, but God answered their prayer with Sarah giving birth to Isaac.   Sarah's joy was made complete in this child, and he is the father of the lineage that led to Jesus of Nazareth.

21

Jacob loved Rachel, but she was unable to give him a child. Her prayers went on for years and she felt humiliated because Jacob's other wives gave him ten sons.   But God is faithful.   God heard her prayers and gave her a son named Joseph.   This same Joseph would save his family from starvation in Egypt.

The list goes on, but the theme is the same.   Not that children are a blessing from God, but God is the blessing who hears our prayers and answers them.

Which is more difficult: to grant a child to a woman who is physically unable to conceive; or to grant your wish for peace in your household … or eternal salvation for your child … or for reconciliation with a loved one where the break seems too horrible to fix?   Our need is defined by the answers to the prayers that come from a faithful God.

> *And consider your relative Elizabeth—even she has conceived a son in her old age, and this is the sixth month for her who was called childless. For nothing will be impossible with God."* **Luke 1:36-37 (HCSB)**

5   PICKING LEADERS

DID YOU KNOW?

We look at people and make judgments based on their appearance.   Sometimes we judge by how well they are dressed; sometimes by their cleanliness; sometimes by their size, height, weight or combination of those.

This is not unusual; we purchase products based on the appearance of the packaging.   We choose political candidates less by what they have done than on how they are marketed.   People get advanced college degrees in marketing to know how to package products (or candidates) to appeal to the targeted market … that's you!

When I was a child I wanted my mom to buy that chocolate puff-ball cereal … not for the cereal (it tasted awful!), but for the secret decoder ring that came inside the box.   Today we pick our leaders for the goodies we think we will get from them after we open the ballot box.   The cereal box is colored to attract the children, not the parents.   The candidates are dressed and presented to reach their "customer"… the voter.   And the voter is as vulnerable as the child in the cereal row.

When God sent Samuel to find a King for Israel, he was warned by God to not look at the appearance of the potential king.   Do not be impressed because he is tall, or good looking.   God reminds Samuel that He knows the man from the INSIDE ...   not from the outer wrapper.

> *When they arrived, Samuel saw Eliab and said, "Certainly the LORD's anointed one is here before Him." But the LORD said to Samuel, "Do not look at his appearance or his stature, because I have rejected him. Man does not see what the LORD sees, for man sees what is visible, but the LORD sees the heart."* ***1 Samuel 16:6-7 (HCSB)***

As God gives us the opportunity to choose our leaders ... for public office or for the church or in the business world ... we would do well to look as God would look.   Resumes tell a distorted story and personal appearance is like a cereal box cover.   Look at the INSIDE.   Pray for God's wisdom before you choose.   God will help you choose if you, like Samuel, will listen to God's direction.

Do you have choices to make?   Be careful which wrapper you choose or you might end up with those puff balls.   Seek wisdom ...see James 1 on finding wisdom.

6   LET THE LORD SPEAK

DID YOU KNOW?

The best and most effective sermon I ever preached came
when I was a youth minister. The pastor stuck his head into
my Sunday school classroom and said, "I have an
emergency to attend to.   You are preaching in twenty
minutes."   Another was at a Christian men's meeting
and the guest speaker didn't show up so I was asked to
speak.   I went to my car to get my Bible and as I came
back in, I was being introduced as the speaker.

My first pastor once told me that if you are truly called to
preach, you don't need three weeks to prepare it.   I didn't
know it at the time, but I have since found this to be a
Biblical truth.

> *Now we have not received the spirit of the world, but
> the Spirit who /comes/ from God, so that we may
> understand what has been freely given to us by God.
> We also speak these things, not in words taught by
> human wisdom, but in those taught by the Spirit,
> explaining spiritual things to spiritual people. **1
> Corinthians 2:12-13 (HCSB)***

When you speak concerning matters of scripture and the
Lord, we would be dishonest to speak the opinion of man.
The fact that there are several pastors who do this on a
regular basis does not justify this.   We are told by our Lord

that there will come a time when we are going to be called to speak concerning matters of faith.   We may even be called before the elders of the church and asked to explain our teachings.   He said we are not to worry about what to say, but to be certain that when that time comes, the Holy Spirit will provide for you the words that are necessary.

> *Whenever they bring you before synagogues and rulers and authorities, don't worry about how you should defend yourselves or what you should say. For the Holy Spirit will teach you at that very hour what must be said."* **Luke 12:11-12 (HCSB)**

The same is to be said for you.   It is not only the ordained minister that this message is for, but to every born-again Christian.   We are all called to share our faith… on a moment's notice.   Don't worry that you are not ready …. God is ready … are you willing?

7   SOLOMON'S FALL

DID YOU KNOW?

Love can get you into trouble.   Of course you know that!
But God told us about it and how we were supposed to avoid
getting into that kind of trouble.   As usual, people didn't
listen in the Old Testament … or in the New Testament ….
or in the present world.

God told the Israelites to stay away from the people who had
been occupying the Promised Land before them.   These
people worshiped false gods and lived in other manners of
wickedness.   If the Israelites were to marry these people,
they would be led into sharing in those practices.
Therefore, avoid them; drive them out of the land; do not go
into their land to find them; do not associate with them.
But, of course, they didn't listen.

> *King Solomon loved many foreign women in addition
> to Pharaoh's daughter: Moabite, Ammonite, Edomite,
> Sidonian, and Hittite women from the nations that the
> LORD had told the Israelites about, "Do not intermarry
> with them, and they must not intermarry with you,
> because they will turn you away [from Me] to their
> gods." Solomon was deeply attached to these women
> and loved [them].* **1 Kings 11:1-2 (HCSB)**

When I was a teenager, my parents were really
unreasonable.   They told me that some of my friends were

not the kind of people that I should be hanging around with and that they would only get me into trouble.   I thought they were totally disconnected with the real world.   Why couldn't they be cool like other parents?   Perhaps they had heard about this guy named Solomon. Most of my childhood friends died at a young age or ended up in jail.   Many others are alcoholics or addicted to other drugs.

Paul tells us not to be unequally yoked.   He means that we should not tie ourselves to people with other beliefs.   Do you suppose he knew about Solomon?

No, I don't mean to be judgmental.   But … do you suppose that my parents might have been onto something?   Do you suppose that God might have been right?   Is there something to be learned from the lesson of Solomon?

Who are you influencing?   Who is influencing you?

8   THE BOSSY BOSS

DID YOU KNOW?

You don't have to be bossy to be a boss.   As a matter of fact, you will be a much more effective leader if you serve your subordinates, rather than expecting them to serve you. This is not some new philosophy; it is a Biblical principle that is well worth looking at.

Rehoboam went to the city of Shechem to be anointed as King.   He felt that being King was his right, but there was another who could have made that claim.   Jeroboam, son of Nebat, came to Rehoboam and offered his loyalty. Rehoboam talked to his top advisors and asked them how he should respond.

> *They replied, "Today if you will be a servant to these people and serve them, and if you respond to them by speaking kind words to them, they will be your servants forever."*   **1 Kings 12:7 (HCSB)**

Rehoboam didn't think that he should be so much a wimp to these folks.   So he went to his younger friends and asked them what he should do,

> *Then the young men who had grown up with him told him, "This is what you should say to these people who said to you, 'Your father made our yoke heavy, but you, make it lighter on us!' This is what you should tell*

them: 'My little finger is thicker than my father's loins!
1 Kings 12:10 (HCSB)

Which advisors would you listen to?   I hope it wouldn't be following Rehoboam's example.   He took the advice of the younger friends.   He so infuriated people that he was killed and Jeroboam was made King in his place.

Perhaps the advice from our Lord Jesus would have been whispered in Rehoboam's ear from across the centuries. Here are two examples of the advice from Jesus to His Apostles:

> *…and whoever wants to be first among you must be your slave;* ***Matthew 20:27 (HCSB)***

> *Sitting down, He called the Twelve and said to them, "If anyone wants to be first, he must be last of all and servant of all."*   ***Mark 9:35 (HCSB)***

The best bosses I have ever had followed this advice.   The worst tried the road of Rehoboam.   Which road to leadership will you follow?

9   SERVING FALSE GODS

DID YOU KNOW?

You can offer sacrifices to rocks. rivers, dogs, stone pillars, and even insects; but if you do you are insulting God and offering your goods to a nothing.   God tells us that there is no other god except Him.   He also demands that we worship no god but Him.   If we should make sacrifices to anything else, we have made that something else a god and we insult the Maker of heaven and earth.

Throughout the history of man, our ancestors have worshipped rivers, snakes, cows, stars, trees, and hand-made statues.   The sad part is that they were worshipping things, and things are created.   God is the Creator.   So instead of worshipping the Creator, they worshipped His creation.   This would be like worshipping the altar of God rather than the god of the altar.

Paul pointed out the foolishness of such false worship.

> *About eating food offered to idols, then, we know that "an idol is nothing in the world," and that "there is no God but one." For even if there are so-called gods, whether in heaven or on earth—as there are many "gods" and many "lords"—*
> *yet for us there is one God, the Father. All things are from Him, and we [exist] for Him. And [there is] one*

*Lord, Jesus Christ. All things are through Him, and we [exist] through Him. **1 Corinthians 8:4-6 (HCSB)***

Although there are many things that become gods to us, a Christian knows that there is but one God and He is Jehovah, the creator of all things including the creator of us.

But the sad part is that we allow other gods in our lives and we even make sacrifices to them.   When we choose to follow our own desires rather than the desires of God, we make ourselves to be above God, and thereby make ourselves into gods.   We sacrifice our wealth on satisfying those desires, contrary to God's wishes.   We are sacrificing to a god that is not a god at all.

> *But if it doesn't please you to worship Yahweh, choose for yourselves today the one you will worship: the gods your fathers worshiped beyond the Euphrates River or the gods of the Amorites in whose land you are living. As for me and my family, we will worship Yahweh." **Joshua 24:15 (HCSB)***

Whom will you serve?

10   IT WON'T KILL YOU

DID YOU KNOW?

Some people get their enjoyment out of convincing other people to rebel against God.   This is true... but why?   It's because sin seems to be more fun than following the Lord.

The devil tells us how much fun it WILL be, but he doesn't mention the price you will have to pay for the momentary pleasures he offers.   Across society, we are told to live it up because "this is as good as it gets."   "Go ahead, it won't kill you!"   But drugs and self-destructive sexual behaviors will, in fact, kill you.

Here is the warning that the Apostle Peter shared with us:

> *But there were also false prophets among the people, just as there will be false teachers among you. They will secretly bring in destructive heresies, even denying the Master who bought them, and will bring swift destruction on themselves.   Many will follow their unrestrained ways, and the way of truth will be blasphemed because of them.* ***2 Peter 2:1-2 (HCSB)***

But here is the really sad part of this.   Knowing that the behavior is self-destructive, some people continue in it, and encourage others to join them in it.   Here is what the Apostle Paul told the Romans.

Although they know full well God's just sentence—that those who practice such things deserve to die—they not only do them, but even applaud others who practice them. **Romans 1:32 (HCSB)**

Be aware of the bandwagon approach as you are being told to what do; they will tell you that "everybody is doing it." These false leaders are the very people Peter and Paul warned us about.

But even the message of "It won't kill you!" is the same as the devil offered in the Garden of Eden when the Serpent told Eve that very lie.   I guess the devil isn't inventive enough to come up with a new line.   Just remember, Eve found out what a liar the devil is… he is the father of lies.   Is that the advice you would follow?

Whose advice do you follow for enjoyment?

Someone Much Greater than I

by Keith A. Rothra

There's a new moon on my horizon.
There's a star up above me in the sky.
And the universe all around me proclaims
There is Someone much greater than I.

There is Someone who put this all together
There is Someone who has the Master
plan
There is Someone who gave this world it's
beauty and
He is Someone much greater than any
man.

There's a child who was born in a manger,
With a star up above Him in the sky,
And the universe all around Him
proclaimed,
There is Someone much greater than I.

He's the Someone who put it all together.
He's the Someone who has the Master
plan
His name is Jesus, He's my Lord and my
Savior and

He is Someone much greater than any
man.

From the grave, He rose up in victory.
He's coming back with the clouds in the
sky.
And the universe all around Him will
proclaim,
This is Someone much greater than I.

He's the Someone who put it all together.
He's the Someone who has the Master
plan
His name is Jesus, He's my Lord and my
Savior and He is Someone much greater than
any man.

11 YOUR OWN UNDERSTANDING

DID YOU KNOW?

You cannot live "on your own."   You need help.

Many people have told me that they don't need anybody; that they can take care of themselves.   I claimed that independent cry for 37 years, and couldn't understand why my life was in such a wreck.   Can I live on my own, without direction? The Bible, the best owner's manual for life, says otherwise.

> *So, whoever thinks he stands must be careful not to fall.* ***1 Corinthians 10:12 (HCSB)***

When you think you need no help in decision making or in contending with the trials of life, you make yourself easy pickings for those who would take advantage of your innocent vulnerability.   Even the greatest human, other than Jesus, could not contend with the wiles of the Devil without Divine protection. The Archangel Michael, the greatest of the warrior angels, dared not rebuke the devil, but called upon the Lord to rebuke him.

The people of Edom thought they were safe. They lived in cliff dwellings where nobody could attack them in their high and lofty perch.   They were like the song writer Paul Simon's "I Am a Rock" ,where he said, "I've built walls … a fortress deep and mighty."   But no person is a rock or an island.   Read what the Lord said to Edom.

> *Your presumptuous heart has deceived you, you who live in clefts of the rock in your home on the heights, who say to yourself, "Who can bring me down to the ground?"* **Obadiah 1:3 (HCSB)**

Oddly, your only hope of victory is to surrender. Give yourself to God.   Submit to His leadership, to His advice, to His Word, to His protection. Lean not upon your own understanding.   My understanding is what got me into the troubles I experienced.   It was the wisdom of the Word of God that brought me out of those swamps.   His advice is clear from the Book of Proverbs.

> *Trust in the LORD with all your heart, and do not rely on your own understanding;* **Proverbs 3:5 (HCSB)**

12   HONORING GOD FIRST

DID YOU KNOW?

God wants total devotion; nothing less than total will be acceptable.   Anything that stands between you and God is an insult to your Lord.   Not just anything, but also anybody.

Asa became King of Judea.   His father and his grandfather had not served the Lord while they had been King.   They had allowed evil practices throughout the kingdom during their reigns, and they had even encouraged people to worship Baal and other false and foreign gods.   When Asa became King, he determined to end those practices and to restore the kingdom to the service of God.

But Asa's mother was still Queen.   She still encouraged these false worship practices.   Asa could not allow even his own mother to continue in this way.   Here is the account from scripture:

> In the twentieth year of Israel's King Jeroboam, Asa became king of Judah and reigned 41 years in Jerusalem. His grandmother's name was Maacah daughter of Abishalom. Asa did what was right in the LORD's eyes, as his ancestor David had done. He banished the male cult prostitutes from the land and removed all of the idols that his fathers had made. He

also removed his grandmother Maacah from being queen mother because she had made an obscene image of Asherah. Asa chopped down her obscene image and burned it in the Kidron Valley. **1 Kings 15:9-13 (HCSB)**

Several centuries later, Jesus demanded it as well. When a wealthy young man came asking Jesus how to inherit the Kingdom of God, Jesus told him to sell all of his possessions and give the money to the poor. The young man could not part with his wealth. Jesus said that material wealth must not be your priority.

Then Jesus addressed even family relationships. Like King Asa, we must put our family into a position of lesser importance than our relationship with Him.

> *"If anyone comes to Me and does not hate his own father and mother, wife and children, brothers and sisters—yes, and even his own life—he cannot be My disciple.* **Luke 14:26 (HCSB)**

Jesus does not mean to HATE your parents, but these words mean to put at a lesser priority. That means to put Jesus before them in importance in your life. Always honor your mother and father, but not greater than you honor the Lord. Love your Lord with all your heart.

13   UNLEARNED TEACHERS

DID YOU KNOW?

There are people teaching Biblical concepts that have no idea what they are teaching.   They teach what they want to believe and use their own interpretations of scripture without having any education in the meaning of the words.

Let me give you an example of this.

> *For Christ is the end of the law for righteousness to everyone who believes.* **Romans 10:4 (HCSB)**

From this verse, some teach that the law ended when Christ came.   This is a logical conclusion for a person who is not schooled in Greek, the language in which the New Testament was written.   Here is what the Greek says.

In Greek, "end" is written "telos", which means PURPOSE.

What this says is: "The Purpose of the law was Christ, resulting in righteousness for everyone who believes."

This concept comes again in 1 Timothy

> *Now the goal of our instruction is love [that comes] from a pure heart, a good conscience, and a sincere faith.* **1 Timothy 1:5 (HCSB)**

But immediately after this scripture comes this, from Paul:

> *Now the goal of our instruction is love [that comes] from a pure heart, a good conscience, and a sincere faith. Some have deviated from these and turned aside to fruitless discussion. They want to be teachers of the law, although they don't understand what they are saying or what they are insisting on.* **1 Timothy 1:5-7 (HCSB)**

Paul is telling us that there will be some who will not follow the law with a pure heart, but will go out and teach their own version of God's word, even when they don't understand the scripture they are trying to teach.

So what are we supposed to do? I would suggest the direction given by Paul to young Timothy.

> *Be diligent to present yourself approved to God, a worker who doesn't need to be ashamed, correctly teaching the word of truth. But avoid irreverent, empty speech, for this will produce an even greater measure of godlessness.* **2 Timothy 2:15-16 (HCSB)**

14 CHRISTIANITY IN GOVERNMENT

DID YOU KNOW?

The government of the United States is based on Judeo-Christian principle.   Many people think that there is a required separation of church and state in our Constitution, but that is not so.   Many aspects of our government were derived from our Christian heritage, since most of our founding fathers were well schooled in Christianity.   The basic principle of our government is a separation of powers which is drawn directly from the Bible.

For example, the President has a short term in which to act on bills passed by Congress.   If the President does nothing before that period lapses, then the bill becomes law without the President's signature.   How long is that period?   It is ten days…. not including Sundays.

Why not Sundays?   Because, in the view of our Christian founders, Sunday is the "Lord's Day" and no work will be done on that day.   If they had been Jewish, it would have been Saturday. If they had been Moslem, they would have chosen Friday.   But they were Christian and so they proclaimed Sunday as a day exempt from work.

James Madison, commonly called "the Father of the Constitution" was a disciple of two great philosophers. One, John Locke, was from England, and the other, Baron Charles Montesquieu, was from France.

Madison and Jefferson borrowed Locke's concept that our rights are from God, not from the government. As Jefferson quoted Locke in the Declaration of Independence,

> *"All men are created equal and are endowed by their Creator with certain unalienable rights."*

From Montesquieu came the three branches of government. The French Baron borrowed this concept from the prophet Isaiah.

> *For the LORD is our Judge, the LORD is our lawgiver, the LORD is our King. He will save us.* ***Isaiah 33:22 (HCSB)***

"The Lord is our Judge" gives us the judicial branch, or the courts.

"The Lord is our Lawgiver" defines the legislative branch, which is Congress.

"The Lord is our King" declares an Executive branch, from which we get our office of the President.

Notice that the center and final authority of all the government, however, is the Lord.

May it ever be so.

*But if it doesn't please you to worship Yahweh,
choose for yourselves today the one you will worship:
the gods your fathers worshiped beyond the
Euphrates River or the gods of the Amorites in whose
land you are living. As for me and my family, we will
worship Yahweh."* **Joshua 24:15 (HCSB)**

15　THE ONE SACRIFICE

DID YOU KNOW?

Prior to the sacrifice of Jesus, the Jewish priests offered massive numbers of sacrifices each year to God.　The law was that there was only one way to pay for sins: a sacrifice of blood.　Each family had to offer a sheep or a goat yearly for their own sins, and the High Priest would offer a heifer for the nation, but not until he had given his own sacrifice for his own sin.　There was a river of blood on the sacrificial altars during the great feasts.

But the blood bath was only good for one year.　Therefore, each year the High Priest and each family had to go back to the temple and do it again; year after year.

But with Jesus as your sacrifice, you are not required to do this.　Jesus died one time for all sin for all men for all time. After He did this, He rose from the grave; but He didn't have to come back and go through it all again in the next year. This was the ultimate sacrifice; it was a sacrifice of the blood of God.　Any further blood sacrifices would be a stench to the Lord's nostrils.　Ever since He came in the person of Jesus of Nazareth and sacrificed Himself on the altar of Calvary, no other sacrifice is necessary.　To try to appease God with further sacrifice would be to reject the sacrifice of Jesus.

> *He entered the most holy place once for all, not by the blood of goats and calves, but by His own blood,*

having obtained eternal redemption.   **Hebrews 9:12 (HCSB)**

How sad it is that there are some who teach that you must do something further to EARN your salvation.   Freedom from your sin has already been bought, and at a very great price.

If someone tells you that you need to do something to pay for your sins, tell them that Jesus already did it, and that you accept that gift of grace He provided for you.   Let us not insult God by telling Him that His sacrifice is insufficient. His grace is sufficient.

16   WHO CREATED THE WORLD?

DID YOU KNOW?

God created everything in the universe.   But Jesus was the Creator.

Most people envision God speaking the earth into existence at the beginning. However, this is the way that scripture reveals creation.

> *In the beginning God created the heavens and the earth.* **Genesis 1:1 (HCSB)**

From this, most believers see God the Father as the Creator. Just imagine God sitting on His eternal throne, as He speaks with a voice that rattles the corners of the universe.   No Big Bang to theorize about; no gaseous explosions that turned into planets and stars; no aliens to plant civilization on this little blue ball in space.   It says that God created the heavens and the earth.   However, read these two statements by Paul and John.

> *For everything was created by Him, in heaven and on earth, the visible and the invisible, whether thrones or dominions or rulers or authorities— all things have been created through Him and for Him.* **Colossians 1:16 (HCSB)**

All things were created through Him, and apart from Him not one thing was created that has been created. **John 1:3 (HCSB)**

Who is "Him?"

He was in the world, and the world was created through Him, yet the world did not recognize Him. He came to His own, and His own people did not receive Him. But to all who did receive Him, He gave them the right to be children of God, to those who believe in His name, **John 1:10-12 (HCSB)**

The "Him" that created all the world was the same "Him" who came and gave His life to save the world… the "Him" was Jesus of Nazareth, our Lord and Savior. His other titles include Messiah, Emmanuel, Lord of Lords, King of Kings, and the Babe of Bethlehem.

That's right. Jesus was the Creator of the world… and of all that is in it … which includes you. That's why He loves you so much.

17   RELATIONSHIPS

DID YOU KNOW?

Christianity is all about relationships.   What is YOUR
Relationship With God?   God WANTS a relationship with you ….
Do you have one?

> *Love consists in this: not that we loved God, but that He*
> *loved us and sent His Son to be the propitiation for our*
> *sins.* ***1 John 4:10 (HCSB)***

In the Garden ….. Adam had a SPECIAL RELATIONSHIP with
God.   He walked in the Garden with God ……. <u>DAILY</u>.   He
TALKED with God …. In a very personal way.   But when Adam
disobeyed God , it broke the relationship.

> *For this is what love for God is: to keep His commands.*
> *Now His commands are not a burden,* ***1 John 5:3 (HCSB)***

ADAM KNEW what he did… so he HID FROM GOD.   Did you
ever find yourself wanting to HIDE FROM GOD? … ASHAMED of
what you have done, and KNOWING that GOD KNOWS.

When You and I disobey God, HE doesn't hide from us …. WE
HIDE FROM GOD!   God comes LOOKING FOR US, Just like He
came looking for Adam!

But a Relationship with God REQUIRES a relationship with other
people.

*And this is love: that we walk according to His commands. This is the command as you have heard it from the beginning: you must walk in love. **2 John 1:6 (HCSB)***

*Pursue peace with everyone, and holiness—without it no one will see the Lord. Make sure that no one falls short of the grace of God and that no root of bitterness springs up, causing trouble and by it, defiling many. **Hebrews 12:14-15 (HCSB)***

How can we live in a peaceful relationship with God, when we have a broken relationship with someone God loves? How can we walk in love with God when we have a broken relationship with God's children?

When you have a broken relationship, does it not HURT ? ? ? Do you not PRAY FOR RESTORATION ? ? ? Do you pray for the other person? ? ? Do you pray for YOUR CONSCIENCE? ? ?

For the one who wants to love life and to see good days must keep his tongue from evil and his lips from speaking deceit, **1 Peter 3:10 (HCSB)**

Husbands ..... LOVE YOUR WIVES
Wives ...... HONOR YOUR HUSBANDS
Parents ..... DO NOT DRIVE YOUR CHILDREN TO WRATH
Children ..... OBEY YOUR PARENTS in the Lord ....
Young people ..... MARRY BEFORE YOU LIVE TOGETHER.

How can you ask God to bless a relationship when you disobey Him as you establish it?

The whole Christian thing is about RELATIONSHIPS. You MUST have a LOVE RELATIONSHIP WITH GOD. You cannot have that relationship if you live in disobedience.

51

You must have a LOVE RELATIONSHIP with your fellow man …You cannot have a relationship with God if you cannot love His child.

You must have a love relationship with your family ….Parents with the children …. Children with the parents …Husband and wife with one another.

What is your relationship with God?

It is NOT a question of "DO YOU BELIEVE IN GOD?"   It is more of a question of "Do you make this God your LORD?"   … and "how can He be LORD if you do not OBEY this LORD?"

Love one another.

18 FREEDOM FROM LEPROSY

DID YOU KNOW?

If you seek Jesus and let Him change you, there is no need to tell others that you have changed. The others will see the changes in you.

Not long after I was saved I visited Hornell NY to see my family there.   I was shocked when my Uncle Leo asked me if I was born again.   I knew that he and my Aunt Robin were believers, and it gave me great joy to share with them that yes, indeed, I was a child of Christ.   I was thrilled that he could see the change in me.

When Jesus healed a man with leprosy, Jesus told the man to tell nobody, but to only go to the priest and have him agree that the leprosy was gone.   Still, the word of the healing quickly spread out to the people.

> *While He was in one of the towns, a man was there who had a serious skin disease all over him. He saw Jesus, fell facedown, and begged Him: "Lord, if You are willing, You can make me clean." Reaching out His hand, He touched him, saying, "I am willing; be made clean," and immediately the disease left him. Then He ordered him to tell no one: "But go and show*

yourself to the priest, and offer what Moses prescribed for your cleansing as a testimony to them." But the news about Him spread even more, and large crowds would come together to hear Him and to be healed of their sicknesses. **Luke 5:12-16 (HCSB)**

If we allow the healing to change us, we will not continue in the same old way. Just as the former leper was made free of his crippling disease, we are made free of our sin. The leper no longer had to be a social outcast; and we no longer need to be limited by our former ways. Go about your new life of freedom, and those who know you will see the changes He has made in you.

Let people see the changes in you. Ask Jesus to release you from your past and walk in your newfound freedom. Others will spread the word about the change God has made in you.

19   BLESSED OR CURSED

DID YOU KNOW?

God is your provider, your protector, your strength.   He expects you to rely on Him, and upon nobody else.   As a matter of fact, He doesn't even want you to rely upon yourself, but to turn to Him for your wisdom in life.

> *Trust in the LORD with all your heart, and do not rely on your own understanding;*   **Proverbs 3:5 (HCSB)**

How many time have you fussed and fumed over some problem in your life and you could not find a solution?   Of course we have all done that, but how far did you go before you finally decided to turn to God for help?   Why is it that God is so often our LAST resort when He tells us that He should be our FIRST.

I have gone to friends for solutions.   The result was usually some pretty bad advice.   When I ask someone for advice on my life, they are no better qualified to solve MY problems than they are to solve their own.   Re-read the previous paragraph to see how good they are at that.   Here is the Lord's opinion of our search for wisdom.

> This is what the LORD says: The man who trusts in mankind, who makes [human] flesh his strength and

turns his heart from the LORD is cursed.   **Jeremiah 17:5 (HCSB)**

God is not telling us to turn away from our friends, but we must remember that the only true source of wisdom is not man, but God.   He is the object of our search.

The man who trusts in the LORD, whose confidence indeed is the LORD, is blessed. **Jeremiah 17:7 (HCSB)**

You can do your own thing of you want, but these verses tell me that I need to rely on more than me; I need to rely on more than friends; I need to rely upon the Lord.   Where do you get your guidance for your daily walk?   It's your choice: blessed or cursed.   Which would you choose?

20 WITCHES AND MEDIUMS

DID YOU KNOW?

With all the movies and television specials dealing with witchcraft, sorcerers, warlocks, and mediums, one would think that this is a normal (although paranormal) behavior. The Bible is very clear about this. What does the Bible say about these behaviors? The Bible says NO.

> *No one among you is to make his son or daughter pass through the fire, practice divination, tell fortunes, interpret omens, practice sorcery, cast spells, consult a medium or a familiar spirit, or inquire of the dead. Everyone who does these things is detestable to the LORD, and the LORD your God is driving out the nations before you because of these detestable things.* **Deuteronomy 18:10-12 (HCSB)**

Harry Potter is a warlock (male witch); the popular movement is about zombies; people are seeking advice from their dead relatives through mediums. The Bible tells us to not allow a witch in our presence, and to not consult with those who consult with the dead. To do these things is to be in direct disobedience to the Word of God.

Consider this: if the mediums and horoscope writers knew what would be happening in the future, would they not be making a killing on Wall Street .... or winning a lot of lotteries?   They are liars and fakes who are called soothsayers because they offer advice to say soothing things to make you happy.   Would you knowingly seek advice from a liar?

So where CAN we go for advice?   ...certainly not to the dead or those consulting with them.   God tells us where to go:

> *Now if any of you lacks wisdom, he should ask God, who gives to all generously and without criticizing, and it will be given to him.* ***James 1:5 (HCSB)***

Instead of seeking advice from the dead, who cannot speak, God tells us to consult with the LIVING GOD.   He sees the future .... However, I wouldn't recommend asking him to give you winning lottery numbers.   But He will give you good advice on how to live in peace and joy.

Go to the real source of wisdom ..... God.

The Voice of Angels

by Keith A. Rothra

not a dream, it's the voice of angels,
Calling me, oh yes, they're calling me.
Saying, "Come! Come to a home that's
eternal."
It's not a dream. It's angels calling me.

I awoke from a sleep fill with angels,
And their voices were just filling the air,
Saying, "Glory to God in the Highest!,"
And, "Peace to His children everywhere."

Then one approached, wearing robes of
white linen,
And it seemed like there were stars in his
hair.
He said, "My child, there's a mansion
prepared just for you,
Believe in Jesus, and I'll see you there."

It's not a dream, it's the voice of angels,
Calling me, oh yes, they're calling me.
Saying, "Come! Come to a home that's
eternal."
It's not a dream. It's angels calling me.
It's not a dream. It's angels calling me.

21 MISSIONARY SUPPORT

DID YOU KNOW?

Our Lord called for missionaries to reach out to the ends of the earth.   I have had the privilege of visiting several countries, but never as a missionary.   Today, I am like many other Christians in that I try to help others to go to those faraway places by contributing financially to their support.

The Lord knows that not everyone will be a missionary in foreign lands.   But some are called to do so.   The others are called to help.   The Apostle John writes about this in 3 John.

> *Dear friend, you are showing faithfulness by whatever you do for the brothers, especially when they are strangers.   They have testified to your love in front of the church. You will do well to send them on their journey in a manner worthy of God, since they set out for the sake of the Name, accepting nothing from pagans. Therefore, we ought to support such men so that we can be coworkers with the truth.* ***3 John 1:5-8 (HCSB)***

Some Christian denominations have special funds to support their missionaries.   Some support missionaries through individual congregations supporting specific workers of the field. Either way, they do a good work. Many are supporting someone they don't know, but trust that the calling of the Lord upon them will be brought to good fruit through this help.

There is a song called "Thank You" which talks about giving to missionaries. People come to know the Lord and lives are changed when we give to this God-ordained work.

When was the last time you helped a missionary? Maybe you are called to be one, and God will call upon us to support your calling. Or maybe our gifts, and yours, will help someone else stand in glory before the Lord.

> *Therefore, we ought to support such men so that we can be coworkers with the truth. 3 John 1:8 (HCSB)*

22   JUDAS WAS A THIEF

DID YOU KNOW?

Money seems to be a necessary tool in the ministry.   The costs of providing a building, teaching materials, utilities, and salaries seems to demand that money has to be a serious consideration in ministry.

This money mentality prevails altogether too often in ministry today, to the point that the push for revenues outpaces the worship and evangelism.   The focus of ministry must be on reaching people, and we must learn to rely upon the Lord to provide the means of financing it.

When Jesus sent out seventy of His disciples to preach, heal, cast out demons, and raise the dead, how much money did He tell them to take with them?

> *Now go; I'm sending you out like lambs among wolves. Don't carry a money-bag, traveling bag, or sandals; don't greet anyone along the road. Whatever house you enter, first say, 'Peace to this household.' If a son of peace is there, your peace will rest on him; but if not, it will return to you. Remain in the same house, eating and drinking what they offer, for the worker is worthy of his wages. Don't be moving from house to house.*   **Luke 10:3-7 (HCSB)**

Jesus knew that there were occasions where He and His disciples would need some cash. Therefore He appointed a treasurer to carry the money bag for them. Who was the one that Jesus appointed as the treasurer? He appointed Judas Iscariot, knowing that Judas was a thief. Jesus was so unconcerned about the money in the ministry that He appointed a thief to hold the money.

> *Then Mary took a pound of fragrant oil—pure and expensive nard—anointed Jesus' feet, and wiped His feet with her hair. So the house was filled with the fragrance of the oil. Then one of His disciples, Judas Iscariot (who was about to betray Him), said, "Why wasn't this fragrant oil sold for 300 denarii and given to the poor?" He didn't say this because he cared about the poor but because he was a thief. He was in charge of the money-bag and would steal part of what was put in it.* **John 12:3-6 (HCSB)**

Put your ministry attention toward sharing the joy of Jesus Christ and don't worry about the money …. Jesus will take care of your ministry's needs.

23 MINISTRY AMONG ANGER

DID YOU KNOW?

Sometimes we get angry; but we are told to not let our anger lead us to sin.

Jesus got angry from time to time. He was angered that people had turned His Father's house into a den of thieves. On that day He cleared the temple with a small whip He fashioned out of rope.

At a different time, Jesus walked into a synagogue and found a man whose hand was paralyzed. Here is how Mark describes this incident

> Now He entered the synagogue again, and a man was there who had a paralyzed hand. In order to accuse Him, they were watching Him closely to see whether He would heal him on the Sabbath He told the man with the paralyzed hand, "Stand before us." Then He said to them, "Is it lawful on the Sabbath to do what is good or to do what is evil, to save life or to kill?" But they were silent. After looking around at them with anger and sorrow at the hardness of their hearts, He told the man, "Stretch out your hand." So he stretched it out, and his hand was restored. **Mark 3:1-5 (HCSB)**

Jesus was angered at the "hardness of their hearts." If the Pharisees judging Him had been unable to understand, Jesus would have understood their ignorance. However, when someone uses the Word of God to justify harm to a person, it is a different story. These people were trying to use God's law to entrap Jesus.

Jesus healed the man while the hypocritical Pharisees watched. In their hardened hearts, they left the synagogue to find a way to end the Lord's ministry.

There are people today who would try to end the ministry that you are called to do. They will tell you that you cannot speak the Name of the Lord in public places, and will even bring lawsuits to stop the spreading of the Gospel. While we may be angered by their hard hearts, do not let them stop your ministry.

Never grow weary of doing what is right. Just as Jesus went on with the healing, so should we go on with bringing joy, healing, and spiritual revival to those around us.

> *They will turn away from hearing the truth and will turn aside to myths. But as for you, be serious about everything, endure hardship, do the work of an evangelist, fulfill your ministry.* ***2 Timothy 4:4-5 (HCSB)***

24 CONFRONTING A FRIEND

DID YOU KNOW?

Sometimes it takes a friend to tell you that you are wrong.

Although it is hard to tell your best friend that they are doing wrong, when you see it, you have an obligation as a friend to confront them confidentially.

The best example of this is the discussion between Nathan and King David concerning David's sinful actions. He had taken another man's wife as his own and had the other man killed to cover up his sin.   So his friend, Nathan, came to him to tell him of his sin.

Rather than tell him directly, Nathan used a parable to show the evil that David had done.   Here is the account of it from scripture:

> So the LORD sent Nathan to David. When he arrived, he said to him: There were two men in a certain city, one rich and the other poor.   The rich man had a large number of sheep and cattle, but the poor man had nothing except one small ewe lamb that he had bought. He raised it, and it grew up, [living] with him and his children. It shared his meager food and drank from his cup; it slept in his arms, and it was like a

66

*daughter to him. Now a traveler came to the rich man, but the rich man could not bring himself to take one of his own sheep or cattle to prepare for the traveler who had come to him. Instead, he took the poor man's lamb and prepared it for his guest. **2 Samuel 12:1-4 (HCSB)***

David didn't understand that Nathan's parable was about him, and pronounced his sentence upon anyone who would do such a thing. Then Nathan told him who did it.

*David was infuriated with the man and said to Nathan: "As the LORD lives, the man who did this deserves to die! Because he has done this thing and shown no pity, he must pay four lambs for that lamb." Nathan replied to David, "You are the man! **2 Samuel 12:5-7 (HCSB)***

At great risk, Nathan went to the King because he could not bear the pain of knowing what his friend was doing. David could have killed Nathan for his brashness. However, he saw his sin and repented to God.

When we see our friends wandering, it is our responsibility to go to them. And if a friend comes to you with this news, follow David's example: don't kill the messenger ....
Repent.

25   RAHAB THE HARLOT

DID YOU KNOW?

God does not always use the pure and pristine to build the Kingdom of God.   It is true that he used a virgin named Mary to give birth to His promised Messiah and Son. However, God has used people of much lower social esteem to fulfill His promises.

When Joshua was about to lead the Israelites across the Jordan into the Promised Land, he first sent some spies to check out the territory.

> *Joshua son of Nun secretly sent two men as spies from the Acacia Grove, saying, "Go and scout the land, especially Jericho." So they left, and they came to the house of a woman, a prostitute named Rahab, and stayed there.* **Joshua 2:1 (HCSB)**

Did you catch that? Where did these men go?   They went to the home of a prostitute.   No, they did not go there to participate in her trade, they went there for a place to spy.

Rahab the Harlot hid the men when the leaders of the City of Jericho discovered that they had entered the city.   She knew that these men were sent from God, and that God had given the land to the Israelites.   Rahab made herself available for the service of God in accomplishing His purposes.

God did not first come to Rahab and demand that she change her ways before she could do anything for Him. But once she served the Living God, she did change her ways and became the grandmother of Boaz, and the great-grandmother of King David.

God wants to use you for His kingdom. He isn't demanding that you change all your bad habits before you begin. Just surrender yourself to doing what God asks of you or leads you to. He will do the rest. He has no harm in mind for you, but wants only your good.

Your life may be as odd as Rahab's; maybe worse, or not as bad .... it doesn't matter in the eyes of God. He wants you, like Rahab, to serve Him.

It changed Rahab the Harlot's life. What will it do for you?

26   SHOWING GOD'S FACE

DID YOU KNOW?

You are expected to wear the face of God.   Yes.   When people look at you, they should see the face of God looking back at them. The ultimate in adoration is emulation … trying to be just like the one you adore.   Do people see God when they see you?

> *If then there is any encouragement in Christ, if any consolation of love, if any fellowship with the Spirit, if any affection and mercy, fulfill my joy by thinking the same way, having the same love, sharing the same feelings, focusing on one goal. Do nothing out of rivalry or conceit, but in humility consider others as more important than yourselves. Everyone should look out not [only] for his own interests, but also for the interests of others. Make your own attitude that of Christ Jesus,* **Philippians 2:1-5 (HCSB)**

What mental picture comes to mind when I say these names …. Montana ... Romo … Manning ... Abraham Lincoln … Martin Luther King … Marylou Retton ….. Jonas Salk ….. Jesus Christ ….

What mental picture is going to come to mind when I mention YOUR name?   Not in YOUR mind ….. In the minds of the people sitting around you.   In the minds of the people where you work… where you shop …. dine …

I heard some testimony at a funeral where someone was thanking the one who died.   The influence he showed changed this person's life.   I have seen that a lot at funerals.

The question that comes to my mind is ….   When it is YOUR TURN to be in that casket …. What will people be saying about YOU?

You are the only chance some people have to see the face of God.   What do they see when they look into your eyes?   What do you see in the morning when YOU look in the mirror?

> *No one has ever seen God. The One and Only Son— the One who is at the Father's side— He has revealed Him.* **John 1:18 (HCSB)**

The WORD of God is not the only way that God shows Himself. We are told in Romans that God is evident in His creation. And we know that WE are part of that creation.

> *No one has ever seen God. If we love one another, God remains in us and His love is perfected in us.* **1 John 4:12 (HCSB)**

> *Dear friend, do not imitate what is evil, but what is good. The one who does good is of God; the one who does evil has not seen God.* **3 John 1:11 (HCSB)**

Go show someone God.

27　EATEN BY LOCUSTS

DID YOU KNOW?

In spite of all the efforts by mankind, the simplest things can become mountains of insurmountable height.　When we think that we are invincible, we are the most vulnerable. Here is what the Lord tells us about our self-sufficiency:

> *So, whoever thinks he stands must be careful not to fall.*　***1 Corinthians 10:12 (HCSB)***

Whenever you think that you are able to make it on your own … that you don't need God …. that you are self-sufficient …. you are in a heap of trouble.　When your riches convince you that you need nothing because you have proven you can fend for yourself ….　God just might have the last laugh.

The people of Old Testament days thought they did not need God.　They thought they were well off and beyond whatever could happen to them.　Then they experienced a catastrophe.

> *What the devouring locust has left, the swarming locust has eaten; what the swarming locust has left, the young locust has eaten; and what the young locust has left, the destroying locust has eaten.* ***Joel 1:4 (HCSB)***

When man thinks he is invulnerable is the point where God can use something as insignificant as a locust to bring him to his knees.   A bug can eat your food, strip your fruit trees, level your cornfield, destroy your vineyard, and eat everything in your storehouse.   Then, you have nothing. Even your home will be invaded by these critters.   There is no protection from them.

When God sends a swarm of locusts your direction, there is not enough Raid or Black Flag spray in the continent to take care of the invasion.   That is when you discover that God can strip your wealth to nothingness with the smallest of His creations.

Keep your faith in the only reliable keeper and protector. Look to God for your food, your home, your health, your strength, and your salvation.   He is the true provider. Those who choose to lean upon their own understanding do so at the risk of being wiped out by something as simple as a bug.

28   IN THE WOMB

DID YOU KNOW?

God has had a plan for you since before He said, "Let there be light."   He created you for a special purpose within His perfect plan.   He says this so beautifully in His call to Jeremiah:

> *The word of the LORD came to me: I chose you before I formed you in the womb; I set you apart before you were born. I appointed you a prophet to the nations.*   **Jeremiah 1:4-5 (HCSB)**

Like Jeremiah, God formed you in the womb with a purpose. What will you do to fulfill God's plan for you?   We can do one of two things: We can ignore God and follow our own will; or we can listen to God and follow His plan for our lives. The first one robs God of His creation, and results in a lifelong fight with your Creator.   The second recognizes God's absolute right to use His creation (you) according to His plan, and results in a life of harmony with God.

This should be a no-brainer for most people, except that many refuse to admit that there is a Creator at all, let alone One who has a right to direct their life.   They tend to choose the first option, much to their sadness.

The purpose for which God has made you is His gift to you. How you respond to that calling can be your gift back to

God.   He does not want you to DIE for Him … He wants you to LIVE for Him.

> *Therefore, brothers, by the mercies of God, I urge you to present your bodies as a living sacrifice, holy and pleasing to God; this is your spiritual worship.*
> **Romans 12:1 (HCSB)**

29   MESSED UP FUNERALS

DID YOU KNOW?

Jesus raised Lazarus from the dead.   Most Christians are familiar with that encounter.   Lazarus had been dead for four days, and Jesus called him out of the grave; and of course, Lazarus came forth as directed.

But that was not the only person Jesus raised from the dead. He seemed to have a regular habit of messing up funerals. He raised a young man and a young girl on separate occasions.   One of them was right in the middle of the funeral march to the grave.

> *Just as He neared the gate of the town, a dead man was being carried out. He was his mother's only son, and she was a widow. A large crowd from the city was also with her.   When the Lord saw her, He had compassion on her and said, "Don't cry."   Then He came up and touched the open coffin, and the pallbearers stopped. And He said, "Young man, I tell you, get up!"   The dead man sat up and began to speak, and Jesus gave him to his mother. **Luke 7:12-15 (HCSB)***

Can you imagine walking with a casket toward the grave when a man comes up and tells the dead person to "get up," and the dead suddenly isn't dead?   But with Jesus, all things are possible.

He is still capable of doing anything that He did then.   That is the good thing about an unchangeable God.   He still heals the sick; He still casts out demons; and He can still raise the dead.

If Jesus can still do all these things, do you suppose He can still save your soul?   Of course He can …if you will let Him. All you need to do is invest into Him the faith that He has already given you.   And you will not have to be raised from the dead …. You will live eternally with Him.

30   THANK YOU NOTES

DID YOU KNOW?

Sending "Thank You" cards seems to be going out of practice.   If someone gave me a gift when I was a child, my mother made sure I wrote a card or letter to the person thanking them for the gift they gave me.   To ignore the gift and the giver is a gross insult to the person who was generous toward you.

But how about this scenario: You do a great act of kindness toward me and I return to you with a basket of fruit as my token of thanks.   Now that sounds more like it.   But I like fruit too, so I am going to pick out the best of the fruit from the basket and send you the ones that are bruised or partially rotted.   Would the basket of damaged fruit be a good token of my gratitude?

If I gave you a dozen eggs instead of fruit, but gave you the old eggs and kept the fresh ones for myself, would that be a good message of thanks?   Of course it would not.

How do we thank God for His many gifts to us?   Do we show our gratitude?   Here is God's complaint:

> "A son honors /his/ father, and a servant his master.
> But if I am a father, where is My honor? And if I am a
> master, where is /your/ fear of Me? says Yahweh of

Hosts to you priests, who despise My name." Yet you ask: "How have we despised Your name?" "By presenting defiled food on My altar." You ask: "How have we defiled You?" When you say: "The LORD's table is contemptible." "When you present a blind /animal/ for sacrifice, is it not wrong? And when you present a lame or sick /animal/, is it not wrong? Bring it to your governor! Would he be pleased with you or show you favor?" asks the LORD of Hosts. **Malachi 1:6-8 (HCSB)**

God deserves our best. Anything less would be an insult to Him. I have seen gifts to the church that were merely things that people wanted to move out of their garage, yet they want a receipt to write the "gift" off as a charity on their taxes.

We should give from the very best … give from the most select … and be joyful at the opportunity to thank God for His boundless provision.

When I Reach Out

By Keith Rothra

Lord, You don't have to move a mountain.
It's enough for me just knowing that You
can.
And when I'm walking through the valleys
'neath the shadows of those hills,
It's enough to know You're there to take
my hand.

And when I reach out, I always find You're
with me.
And when I reach out, You prove that You
still care.
In those valleys, or on the hilltops,
Whatever life should bring to bear,
When I reach out, I always find You there.

Lord, I know for You there are no burdens,
But for me, sometimes they're all that I can
stand.
I want to thank You, Lord, for caring
You take the crosses I can't bear.
And it's enough to know You're there to
take my hand

And when I reach out, I always find You're
with me.
And when I reach out, You prove that You
still care.
In those valleys, or on the hilltops,
Whatever life should bring to bear,
When I reach out, I always find You there.

31   SEEING GOD'S FACE

DID YOU KNOW?

Most people believe that if you see God, you will die. Moses was warned to tell the people to not try to see God, lest they die.

> *The LORD directed Moses, "Go down and warn the people not to break through to see the LORD; otherwise many of them will die. **Exodus 19:21 (HCSB)***

However, when God wanted the leaders of the Israelites to come to Him, He told Moses to bring them.

> *Then Moses went up with Aaron, Nadab, and Abihu, and 70 of Israel's elders, and they saw the God of Israel. Beneath His feet was something like a pavement made of sapphire stone, as clear as the sky itself.   God did not harm the Israelite nobles; they saw Him, and they ate and drank. **Exodus 24:9-11 (HCSB)***

People feared the very thought of looking at God.   Then He came to earth in the person of Jesus of Nazareth.   And from that day forward, "Whoever calls upon the Name of the Lord shall be saved."

The apostle Phillip told Jesus that it would be sufficient if Jesus would show them God.   Jesus' answer must have been astounding to them:

> *"If you know Me, you will also know My Father. From now on you do know Him and have seen Him."*
> *"Lord," said Philip, "show us the Father, and that's enough for us."   Jesus said to him, "Have I been among you all this time without your knowing Me, Philip? The one who has seen Me has seen the Father. How can you say, 'Show us the Father'?* **John 14:7-9 (HCSB)**

Today, believers in Jesus can look forward to seeing God. You can stand before His throne without fear or even concern.   All you need to do is confess with your own mouth that Jesus is your Lord, and believe in your heart that He is raised from the dead, and you will be saved.   But without Him, you will not like standing in front of the throne of God.   It will be a truly frightening experience.

He stands at your door and knocks.   If you will open up and let Him in, He will come in and sit and eat with you.   No fear.   No condemnation.   No sins to be remembered. Just you and the Lord who calls you friend.

32   SAUL'S DEATH

DID YOU KNOW?

The Amalekites were a nation who, without reason, attacked the Israelites when they came out of Egypt.   Years later, God told King Saul to kill all the Amalekites; kill the men, women, children, the infants, and even the livestock.   King Saul did not do as he was told… he left some to live.   In the end, this disobedience was fatal to King Saul.   The man who killed Saul several years later was an Amalekite. King Saul was killed by a man that Saul would have killed if he had followed God's orders.

On the last day of his life, Saul knew he was surrounded by his enemies and he tried to kill himself with his own spear; but he only severely wounded himself.   Then an Amalekite, who was in the field of battle to collect spoils of war from the fallen, happened upon King Saul.   Saul is leaning against his own spear that he had impaled himself upon.   Saul cried out to him for help.   He asked the Amalekite to kill him before the enemy could find him.   So the man, whom Saul should have killed, killed Saul.

The Amalekite's testimony is found in scripture:

> *"I happened to be on Mount Gilboa," he replied, "and there was Saul, leaning on his spear. At that very moment the chariots and the cavalry were closing in*

on him.   When he turned around and saw me, he called out to me, so I answered: I'm at your service. He asked me, 'Who are you?' I told him: I'm an Amalekite. Then he begged me, 'Stand over me and kill me, for I'm mortally wounded, but my life still lingers.'   So I stood over him and killed him because I knew that after he had fallen he couldn't survive." 2 Samuel 1:6-10 (HCSB)

Do we second guess God?   Saul did, and it cost him his life.   Are there things we are supposed to do but we decide to do it in a different way?   Of course there are!   What can be the result of your disobedience?   Could it cost you your life?   Rather than finding out, do it God's way the first time.

33   TRAIN UP A CHILD

DID YOU KNOW?

What should we teach our children?

They should never be told about our founding fathers or past Presidents.   They need to find out about these things for themselves.   We shouldn't try to influence them.

Likewise, math is one of those things that make some things bigger and better than others.   Children should decide these things for themselves and choose which is better: two or three … or if there even is a two or three.

And bathing is a matter of choice.   All hygiene, for that matter, should be left up to the child to develop his/her own attitude on brushing teeth or hair, or washing.   Their social experience will guide them.

Then there is this thing about a god.   IS there one, or not?   Should it be the parents' right to program their children into such matters?   After all, isn't this also something they should decide for themselves as they mature?

What parent would agree with the first three concepts?   I would hope the number would be few.   And yet I have heard the last one so often from well-meaning parents; even some who profess to be Christians.

Let me share a few tokens from our Lord on the matter:

> *Tell your children about it, and let your children tell their children, and their children the next generation.* **Joel 1:3 (HCSB)**

> *Then Joshua set up in Gilgal the 12 stones they had taken from the Jordan, and he said to the Israelites, "In the future, when your children ask their fathers, 'What is the meaning of these stones?' you should tell your children, 'Israel crossed the Jordan on dry ground.'* **Joshua 4:20-22 (HCSB)**

> *He commanded our fathers to teach to their children* [6] *so that a future generation— children yet to be born— might know. They were to rise and tell their children so that they might put their confidence in God and not forget God's works, but keep His commands.* **Psalm 78:5-7 (HCSB)**

To let a child decide how he/she will respond to God without direction is to turn the child loose in a field of wolves. Such a parent will be held accountable even more than the social system would hold them if they refused to teach their child to bathe.

> *Teach a youth about the way he should go; even when he is old he will not depart from it.* **Proverbs 22:6 (HCSB)**

34   COMPLACENCY

DID YOU KNOW?

Complacency is a very dangerous disease.   It can rob you of the rewards that God has in store for you.   It can create a sense of euphoria where you think that things are going so good that I don't have to do any more.   It tells you, "I can coast for a while."

I just watched a very good college football team fall victim to complacency.   They were playing in a game that they had earned the right to be in.   Their winning record put them among the top teams in the nation.   They had high hopes at a crack at the national championship.   They were really that good.

They got to where they were over twenty points ahead. From here on, all they needed to do was hang on and cruise to victory.   So instead of going after their foe, they sat back and let the foe come at them.   They watched for too long. They lost the game and all hope for the championship was out the window … because they were so good … that they got complacent.

God does not want you to get complacent about your faith. At what point have you done "enough?"   At what point are you so secure that you can let the enemy attack you and you can just sit back and cruise on into heaven?

The team I spoke of got into the bowl games … but they didn't get first prize.   And neither will you get the first prize. Oh, you can get into heaven, "but greater shall be your reward," is the caution given to us by our Savior.

Moses and his people escaped Egypt.   They learned how to live in the desert.   They got comfortable.   But God had something better in mind for them.   He told them,

> *"The LORD our God spoke to us at Horeb: 'You have stayed at this mountain long enough."*
> **Deuteronomy 1:6 (HCSB)**

He told them that it was time to move on to a better place.

Every day is the start of a new opportunity.   Every day is the start of a new year.   Last year is over and gone … with all of its great victories.   You cannot live on that mountain anymore.   There are souls to save … There are needy who must be served …. There are lives to change. This is no time for complacency.

35 WHY CHRISTMAS?

DID YOU KNOW?

Why do we do Christmas?

Perhaps we need to begin with this reminder from God's word.

> *Then God said, "Let Us make man in Our image, according to Our likeness. They will rule the fish of the sea, the birds of the sky, the livestock, all the earth, and the creatures that crawl on the earth." **Genesis 1:26 (HCSB)***

But after He created all of this, man became so totally corrupted that He had to destroy nearly all of it.   He saved only eight people.

When those people survived His destructive flood, they didn't get too many generations down the road before the people tried to become their own gods, and they tried to build a tower to heaven at Babel.   God destroyed the tower and divided the people by languages … and dispersing the around the earth.

> *For I know the plans I have for you"—[this is] the LORD's declaration—"plans for [your] welfare, not for disaster, to give you a future and a hope. **Jeremiah 29:11 (HCSB)***

It didn't work … as He knew it wouldn't.   Some people in the cities of Sodom and Gomorrah were so totally corrupted that ….. well, listen to how He tells it through Peter

> and [if] He reduced the cities of Sodom and Gomorrah to ashes and condemned them to ruin, making them an example to those who were going to be ungodly; **2 Peter 2:6 (HCSB)**

Still, His people rebelled against Him.   He had given them hand written rules about how to live with Him … but they twisted the rules or just outright ignored them.

> The LORD is good to everyone; His compassion [rests] on all He has made. **Psalm 145:9 (HCSB)**

After several centuries of this, He decided that He had to fix what mankind could not fix … man's sinful nature that would lead them into eternal damnation.   He decided to send His own Son to fix the problem.

Which gets us back to the original question.   Why Christmas?

> "For God loved the world in this way: He gave His One and Only Son, so that everyone who believes in Him will not perish but have eternal life. **John 3:16 (HCSB)**

That's why.

36   LIGHT OF THE WORLD

DID YOU KNOW?

I often tell people to take care to share Jesus with people, and to use words if they have to.   But how do you share Jesus without using words?   The answer to that lies in some of the words that Jesus shared with His apostles, followers, and even those who hated Him.

Have you ever been in total darkness?   In Mammoth Cave or Carlsbad Caverns you can experience total darkness. They usually turn off the lights for a tour group inside the caves.   You literally cannot see your hand in front of your face.   To be lost in that cave without light would probably be fatal.

Many people are completely blind, spiritually, and are stumbling in darkness.   They cannot find their spiritual way because they have no light.

> *Then Jesus spoke to them again: "I am the light of the world. Anyone who follows Me will never walk in the darkness but will have the light of life." **John 8:12 (HCSB)***

As the man without light cannot find his way out of the darkness, a person without Jesus cannot find their way out of spiritual blindness.   But with Jesus as their Savior, they can see the way to go.

There is more to this because you can help others shed the scales of spiritual darkness and walk in the light. Just as Jesus is the light of the world, He also told us that we are the light of the world.

> *"You are the light of the world. A city situated on a hill cannot be hidden. No one lights a lamp and puts it under a basket, but rather on a lampstand, and it gives light for all who are in the house. In the same way, let your light shine before men, so that they may see your good works and give glory to your Father in heaven.* **Matthew 5:14-16 (HCSB)**

When you have the "light" of Jesus within, you cannot hide it and be effective for God's Kingdom. Let the world see that light. Show people the light, and use words if you have to.

37 THE COPY CAT TRINITY

DID YOU KNOW?

The devil, Satan, is not very inventive. As a matter of fact, it is pretty difficult to find a single thing that he does that is not a copy of things that the Lord had already done.

God established the Trinity. He is three beings in one: He is God the Father; He is God the son, Jesus; and He is God, the Holy Spirit. The Son, Jesus, could do nothing of Himself, but only what the Father told Him to do. He told us that:

> *"I can do nothing on My own. I judge only as I hear, and My judgment is righteous, because I do not seek My own will, but the will of Him who sent Me.* ***John 5:30 (HCSB)***

The purpose of the Holy Spirit is to draw us to Christ, and keep us there as a sanctified being.

> *By reading this you are able to understand my insight about the mystery of the Messiah. This was not made known to people in other generations as it is now revealed to His holy apostles and prophets by the Spirit:* ***Ephesians 3:4-5 (HCSB)***

Satan has established himself as a god. In Revelation, John refers to him as the Dragon. But the Dragon has appointed his messiah, and even wounded him to death and healed him.

> *And I saw a beast coming up out of the sea. He had 10 horns and seven heads. On his horns were 10 diadems, and on his heads were blasphemous names. The beast I saw was like a leopard, his feet were like a bear's, and his mouth was like a lion's mouth. The dragon gave him his power, his throne, and great authority.* **Revelation 13:1-2 (HCSB)**

But he also created his version of the Holy Spirit.

> *Then I saw another beast coming up out of the earth; he had two horns like a lamb, but he sounded like a dragon. He exercises all the authority of the first beast on his behalf and compels the earth and those who live on it to worship the first beast, whose fatal wound was healed.* **Revelation 13:11-12 (HCSB)**

So Satan, the copycat will set up his own blasphemous trinity. They will appear in the final days. Do not be misled by the copycat god.

38 ENTERTAINING ANGELS

DID YOU KNOW?

There are some Christian churches today that would not welcome Jesus if He were to walk in the door.   The extent of the welcome might be based on the way He is dressed, and perhaps a beard may be the taboo to exclude Him.

In one church I pastored, a young man came to our church fearing he would be rejected again, just like he had been at a previous congregation.   This young man had been involved in satanic worship for three years, sacrificing stolen cats and dogs to Satan in the woods near town.   He began having spiritual experiences that scared him and two of his friends, so he brought the friends to a local church to see if they could get answers.

They were not dressed for most congregations; all three were in black, had long dyed jet-black hair, one had a 3-inch dragon earring and another had an upside-down cross for an earring.   When they came into the church and sat in the back row, they were spotted by two modern-day Pharisees who disapproved of their appearance.

The two men went to the boys and told them that they had no respect for God showing up in a church dressed that way.

They were quickly ushered out the door.   They came for spiritual answers and were thrown out without even being asked why they were there.   The one who came to my church a few weeks later got his answers; he was welcomed and asked by one family to sit with them.

I had the joy of baptizing that young man a couple months later after he renounced his Satanism and accepted Jesus as his Savior and Lord.   His two friends were so turned off by the first church that they didn't want to risk going into another.

> *My brothers, do not show favoritism as you hold on to the faith in our glorious Lord Jesus Christ. For example, a man comes into your meeting wearing a gold ring and dressed in fine clothes, and a poor man dressed in dirty clothes also comes in. If you look with favor on the man wearing the fine clothes and say, "Sit here in a good place," and yet you say to the poor man, "Stand over there," or, "Sit here on the floor by my footstool," haven't you discriminated among yourselves and become judges with evil thoughts?* **James 2:1-4 (HCSB)**

Love conquers where religion enslaves.

> *Let brotherly love continue. Don't neglect to show hospitality, for by doing this some have welcomed angels as guests without knowing it.* **Hebrews 13:1-2 (HCSB)**

39   GIDEON THE WIMP

DID YOU KNOW?

I think we each, at one time or another, have been asked to do something that we were certain we were not capable of doing?   .

Gideon had that experience; but the one calling him was the LORD.   Look at this conversation.

> Then the Angel of the LORD appeared to him and said: "The LORD is with you, mighty warrior."   Gideon said to Him, "Please Sir, if the LORD is with us, why has all this happened? And where are all His wonders that our fathers told us about? They said, 'Hasn't the LORD brought us out of Egypt?' But now the LORD has abandoned us and handed us over to Midian." The LORD turned to him and said, "Go in the strength you have and deliver Israel from the power of Midian. Am I not sending you?" He said to Him, "Please, Lord, how can I deliver Israel? Look, my family is the weakest in Manasseh, and I am the youngest in my father's house." "But I will be with you," the LORD said to him. "You will strike Midian down /as if it were/ one man." **Judges 6:12-16 (HCSB)**

When God decides to call someone, it isn't usually the most qualified.   Paul was a killer of Christians.   Moses was a murderer, too, and he was unable to speak well.   This didn't stop God with either of them.　God equipped them and set them to their called task.

So it was with Gideon.　When Gideon said, "You have the wrong guy, God.　I'm obviously not the man you're looking for," was when God answered with, "Am not I sending you?"

When God calls you to a task, He is not looking for the one who is best equipped,　He has decided whom to equip. That might be the horrible Saul of Tarsus; it might be a stutterer named Moses; it might be a little guy named Gideon who is hiding under a winepress; or it might be you.

Are you able to do what God wants of you?　Of course not; because God doesn't want you to do it; God wants to do it through you.　Let God empower you … and answer, "Here I am, Lord, send me."

40   WAIT UPON THE LORD

DID YOU KNOW?

It is good advice to "wait upon the Lord."   Impatience is the basis for some of the worst of human circumstances.   It is the way of man to want to do God's work for Him because God seems to be procrastinating on what we think needs to be done.

We all know the story of Abraham, who was promised a son who would carry on the seed of Abraham for generations to come.   In that account, Abraham knew that his wife was too old to bear children; even Sarah, his wife knew it was an impossible situation.   So the wise patriarch Abraham took matters into his own hands.   His wife gave him her handmaiden for him to have a child.   When that child, Ishmael, was born, a terrible split opened in the family between the two women.

The rift got even worse when God arranged for Sarah, at 90 years old, to bear a child for Abraham.   The new child, Isaac, was God's chosen; the first child, Ishmael, was not. The split between Isaac's descendants and Ishmael's descendants is the basis of the current battle between the Jews and the Moslems.

There was another, later story of impatience. It involved King Saul, of Israel, and the need to make a sacrifice of a burnt offering. Only the priests can make such a sacrifice, but Samuel the priest didn't come as promised, so Saul ignored God's requirement for who could make the sacrifice, and did it himself.

> *(Saul) waited seven days for the appointed time that Samuel had set, but Samuel didn't come to Gilgal, and the troops were deserting him. So Saul said, "Bring me the burnt offering and the fellowship offerings." Then he offered the burnt offering. Just as he finished offering the burnt offering, Samuel arrived. So Saul went out to greet him, and Samuel asked, "What have you done?" Samuel said to Saul, "You have been foolish. You have not kept the command which the LORD your God gave you. It was at this time that the LORD would have permanently established your reign over Israel, but now your reign will not endure.* **1 Samuel 13:7-14 (HCSB)**

Waiting upon the Lord is always good advice. Impatience with the Lord is never good advice.

If you have a need and are tired of waiting for God's answer …. What are you going to do? For Saul, it only cost him a kingdom; for Abraham, it cost a 4000-year war. What are you going to do?

Praise His Name
By Keith Rothra

You Know, you gotta praise His Name!
You gotta get down on your knees and claim,
All of those things that Jesus has for you (He has for you)
If you want to claim His grace,
It ought to shine right out of your face.
If you want to walk and talk with Jesus, praise His Name.

I heard about a paraplegic,
You can read about him in the Bible,
When Jesus touched and healed that man,
They broke out in revival!

You Know, you gotta praise His Name!
You gotta get down on your knees and claim,
All of those things that Jesus has for you (He has for you)
If you want to claim His grace,
It ought to shine right out of your face.
If you want to walk and talk with Jesus, praise His Name.

I heard about a battle "tween David,
And a giant who was ten feet tall.
Everybody said, "David's good as dead!"
But David never worried at all!

You Know, you gotta praise His Name!
You gotta get down on your knees and claim,
All of those things that Jesus has for you (He has for you)

If you want to claim His grace,
It ought to shine right out of your face.
If you want to walk and talk with Jesus, praise His Name.

41   FEAR OF THE LORD

DID YOU KNOW?

It does not take a village to raise a child … it takes a parent to raise a child.   Yes, the village will influence the child, but the guidance that a child receives from the parent is what will form the behavior for future years.

Solomon's advice to his child is good for any parent to pass on to their own.

> Listen, my son, to your father's instruction, and don't reject your mother's teaching, for they will be a garland of grace on your head and a [gold] chain around your neck. **Proverbs 1:8-9 (HCSB)**

We are also told this:

> Teach a youth about the way he should go; even when he is old he will not depart from it. **Proverbs 22:6 (HCSB)**

I watch parents with a level of fear for our future.   It isn't just the "modern" parents, because it was the same with some when I was young.   I knew of a young man who got on a bull dozer and, after getting it started, drove it up and down a pile of crushed rock until the pile caved in on him. The parents blamed the owner of the equipment.   If the bull dozer had been safely secured, then their child would not have been endangered.

Who would be at fault here????   Would it be the equipment owner who had his bull dozer parked on his own property? .... Or might it be the fault of a child who was needed to be taught to stay off from other people's property, and certainly do not start and drive their heavy equipment?

Let us look at another bit of wisdom from Solomon ...

> *The fear of the LORD is the beginning of knowledge; fools despise wisdom and discipline.* **Proverbs 1:7 (HCSB)**

Parents have the responsibility to teach their children that the world is not theirs to destroy.   Failure to do so is to disregard the Biblical mandates.   As parents ... and grandparents ... the children are our legacy.   To guard them from discipline is to hate the children.   The result of ignoring our responsibility is also foretold.

> *He will die because there is no discipline, and be lost because of his great stupidity.* **Proverbs 5:23 (HCSB)**

Love your children ... give them a love for the Lord.   Train them up in the way they should go.

42   PRAYING FIRE FROM THE SKY

DID YOU KNOW?

Faith can bring fire from the sky.   The prophet Elijah called upon God to consume his offering with fire and God did it in front of hundreds of witnesses.   He used this act of faith to show the falsehood of placing faith in false gods such as Baal.

> Then Elijah said to the prophets of Baal, "Since you are so numerous, choose for yourselves one bull and prepare it first. Then call on the name of your god but don't light the fire."
> So they took the bull that he gave them, prepared it, and called on the name of Baal from morning until noon, saying, "Baal, answer us!" But there was no sound; no one answered. Then they danced, hobbling around the altar they had made.
> At noon Elijah mocked them. He said, "Shout loudly, for he's a god! Maybe he's thinking it over; maybe he has wandered away; or maybe he's on the road. Perhaps he's sleeping and will wake up!"
> They shouted loudly, and cut themselves with knives and spears, according to their custom, until blood gushed over them. All afternoon they kept on raving until the offering of the evening sacrifice, but there

was no sound; no one answered, no one paid attention. **1 Kings 18:25-29 (HCSB)**

When you call on a false god, there is no response.   But when you call on the real one you can expect results.

> *At the time for offering the [evening] sacrifice, Elijah the prophet approached [the altar] and said, "Yahweh, God of Abraham, Isaac, and Israel, today let it be known that You are God in Israel and I am Your servant, and that at Your word I have done all these things.*
> *Answer me, LORD! Answer me so that this people will know that You, Yahweh, are God and that You have turned their hearts back." Then Yahweh's fire fell and consumed the burnt offering, the wood, the stones, and the dust, and it licked up the water that was in the trench. When all the people saw it, they fell facedown and said, "Yahweh, He is God! Yahweh, He is God!"* **1 Kings 18:36-39 (HCSB)**

Elijah knew that God would be exalted by this.   His faithfulness to God and his faith in God was answered by a clear response.   The response discredited Baal; it lifted high the worship of Jehovah, the only real God.

Imagine the embarrassment of Elijah if God had not responded.   But that idea never entered Elijah's mind.   He knew that God would hear his prayer.

Do you know that God will answer your prayers just as readily?   It takes faith.   Do you have faith enough to ask?

43   ONLY LOVE REMAINS

DID YOU KNOW?

One day there will be no hope; in that day there will also no longer be any faith.

I know that many folks, perhaps you among them, think we are already there.   There is hate among the people and many see no future for themselves or for their children.   But I am asking you to look at the "Love Chapter," which is found in 1 Corinthians 13.

The Apostle Paul tells us that one day we will see this …

> And now these three remain: faith, hope and love. But the greatest of these is love. *1 Cor. 13:13 (NIV)*

Do you have faith that God is true to His promise?   He promised us that if you will only believe in His Son, Jesus Christ, then you will have everlasting life.   Do you believe that?   And on what do you base that belief?   You probably believe it through faith in the scripture of John 3:16

> "For God loved the world in this way: He gave His One and Only Son, so that everyone who believes in Him will not perish but have eternal life. *John 3:16 (HCSB)*

But remember this from Hebrews:

> Now faith is the reality of what is hoped for, the proof of what is not seen. *Hebrews 11:1 (HCSB)*

There are two important words found here: Faith and Hope.

You have FAITH that your HOPE of eternal life will be kept through the LOVE of God.

If you stand in that faith, you will one day stand before the throne of God, and that HOPE will be fulfilled.   There will be no more need for HOPE.   And your FAITH will be replaced by what is seen …. There will be no more need for FAITH.

What will remain is the love of God which is what you had faith and hope for all along.   But of the three, faith, hope and love, only the LOVE remains … and it will continue forever.

> *Love never ends. But as for prophecies, they will come to an end; as for languages, they will cease; as for knowledge, it will come to an end.* ***1 Corinthians 13:8 (HCSB)***

> *Now these three remain: faith, hope, and love. But the greatest of these is love.* ***1 Corinthians 13:13 (HCSB)***

Faith will no longer be needed.   Hope will have turned into reality.   But the love of God remains forever.

44   MAKING PROMISES

DID YOU KNOW?

We must be very careful in making promises to God. Oaths are binding things, and an oath to anyone should be kept, but failure to keep your oath to God is specifically mentioned in scripture.

> *When a man makes a vow to the LORD or swears an oath to put himself under an obligation, he must not break his word; he must do whatever he has promised.* **Numbers 30:2 (HCSB)**

However, these vows must be made with great care.   Take for example the vow that was taken by Jephthah in the Book of Judges:

> *Jephthah made this vow to the LORD: "If You will hand over the Ammonites to me, whatever comes out of the doors of my house to greet me when I return in peace from the Ammonites will belong to the LORD, and I will offer it as a burnt offering."* **Judges 11:30-31 (HCSB)**

Jephthah was seeking the hand of God as he was pursuing his enemy, the Ammonites.   His promise to God was that he would kill whatever came out of his house upon his return home, if only God would help in this conquest.

God heard his prayer, and answered the call for help.   But Jephthah surely never thought what this vow might require of him.   He found out when he got home.

> *Judges 11:34-35 (HCSB)* *When Jephthah went to his home in Mizpah, there was his daughter, coming out to meet him with tambourines and dancing! She was his only child; he had no other son or daughter besides her.   When he saw her, he tore his clothes and said, "No! [Not] my daughter! You have devastated me! You have brought great misery on me. I have given my word to the LORD and cannot take [it] back."*

Scripture does not show any time that God has required anyone to sacrifice their child.   God has clearly spoken against this very thing, condemning those who sacrificed their children in the Kidron Valley.

Jephthah, scripture says, fulfilled his promise.   It does not say how it was done.

The key here is that we must each be very cautious about the things we promise to God, or to anyone.   Your word is your honor.   People will read your honesty by the way you keep your promises.   Your witness as a Christian is at stake with every promise you make.

45 TEMPTATION OF JESUS

DID YOU KNOW?

When Jesus was tempted by the Devil in the desert, both He and the Devil were intended to be there; it was for the express purpose of giving the Devil another defeat at the hands of the Son of God.

> *Then Jesus returned from the Jordan, full of the Holy Spirit, and was led by the Spirit in the wilderness for 40 days to be tempted by the Devil.* **Luke 4:1-2 (HCSB)**

Following Jesus' baptism in the Jordan River, He was proclaimed by the Holy Spirit to be the Son of God and the Messiah, and that same Spirit led Jesus out to the desert for the very purpose of the temptation.

If you read on, you will find that the Devil didn't do well in that confrontation. Jesus defeated the temptation in every attempt. He quoted scripture back at Satan with every challenge ….

> *He (Jesus) ate nothing during those days, and when they were over, He was hungry. The Devil said to Him, "If You are the Son of God, tell this stone to become bread." But Jesus answered him, "It is*

*written: Man must not live on bread alone." **Luke 4:2-4 (HCSB)***

*The Devil said to Him, "I will give You their splendor and all this authority, because it has been given over to me, and I can give it to anyone I want. If You, then, will worship me, all will be Yours." And Jesus answered him, "It is written: Worship the Lord your God, and serve Him only." **Luke 4:6-8 (HCSB)***

….. until the Devil tried to reverse the tactic by using scripture against Jesus to entrap Him.   How do you entrap God by using scripture written BY God?

*So he took Him to Jerusalem, had Him stand on the pinnacle of the temple, and said to Him, "If You are the Son of God, throw Yourself down from here. For it is written: He will give His angels orders concerning you, to protect you, and they will support you with their hands, so that you will not strike your foot against a stone." And Jesus answered him, "It is said: Do not test the Lord your God." **Luke 4:9-12 (HCSB)***

Jesus reversed it back again with another scripture quote.

This same Jesus tells you to rely upon the Lord rather than accept or fight temptation.   He told us to pray to Him, "Lead us not into temptation, but deliver us from evil."   His Holy Spirit will always be there to deliver you just as the Holy Spirit delivered Him.

46   THE CASE FOR FAITH

DID YOU KNOW?

Your soul is not saved or lost by the things that you have done … or not done.   Your soul is saved through the price paid by Jesus on the cross of Calvary.   God, in His infinite grace, decided that He would not hold you accountable for your sins if you would put your faith in Jesus.

> *For you are saved by grace through faith, and this is not from yourselves; it is God's gift— **Ephesians 2:8 (HCSB)***

But if it takes God's grace and your faith to be saved, how do we get there?   God's grace is by His will, not ours.   He chose you; you didn't choose Him.   But as to the faith, it is yours, but you can't go to Wal-Mart and buy three pounds of it.   You can only get faith from God   In that previous verse, notice that the faith is not from yourself, but it is a gift of God.   And like all gifts, it cannot be earned …. only freely given.

So what is this thing called faith?   Did you know that there is one chapter in the Bible called "the faith chapter?"   It is the eleventh chapter of Hebrews.   This chapter gives several examples of faith in action, but it begins with a definition of what faith is.

> *Now faith is the reality of what is hoped for, the proof of what is not seen.   **Hebrews 11:1 (HCSB)***

Those things you can see are evident because you can see them.   But who has ever seen God?   Though we have not seen Him, we believe in Him; we believe that He is and that He will do what He has promised.   That is called faith.

I would recommend that you read Hebrews chapter 11.   I also recommend that you read Lee Stroeble's book, The Case for Faith.

Here is the bottom line.   Ask God for faith.   Ask God for even greater faith than you have.   He will bless you, but you must have faith to believe that He will.   This is how your soul is saved, and this is how you will find a more abundant life. Just believe .... and ask.

47   SHARE YOUR JOY

DID YOU KNOW?

Jesus has performed some pretty incredible miracles.   He healed people of their leprosy, gave sight to the blind, raised people from the dead, restored physical strength to cripples, cast out demons, and the list goes on.

What would you do if Jesus restored your hearing when you had been deaf for years?   Would you keep it to yourself so you could secretly listen to people and see who is talking about you?   That might be fun.

What if you had stage four cancer and suddenly you were cancer free?   I have seen this happen, and in some cases the doctors gave God the credit; in other cases, they said that there was "no explanation" for it.   When God does this, He should be given full credit for His work.

There was a man of the Gerasenes who was filled with demons.   He couldn't even be restrained by chains… he broke them away.   But Jesus sent the demons into a herd of pigs.   The man was extremely grateful, and wanted to follow Jesus as the Lord got into His boat to leave.

> *As He was getting into the boat, the man who had been demon-possessed kept begging Him to be with Him.* **Mark 5:18 (HCSB)**

116

Does God want you to go to Him following your healing? … or would He rather you go share the wonders of what He has done for you?

> But He would not let him; instead, He told him, "Go back home to your own people, and report to them how much the Lord has done for you and how He has had mercy on you." **Mark 5:19 (HCSB)**

God wants us to go to the world and tell all about the power available through a relationship with Him. When we do, God's Kingdom grows. Sharing your experiences makes people turn their faith to Him and come to know His amazing grace.

> So he went out and began to proclaim in the Decapolis how much Jesus had done for him, and they were all amazed. **Mark 5:20 (HCSB)**

God wants us to be in this world spreading the Word to others. He will call you home at the time that He knows is best. Until then, share all the miracles you have experienced. They need to know.

48   SWALLOWED BY THE EARTH

DID YOU KNOW?

God has the ability to open the earth and let it swallow you. He not only has the ability, He has a record of doing it. When people have risen up in rebellion against Him, God has opened the earth beneath them, and then He closed it again.

In the wilderness of the Sinai, there arose a group of grumblers who were not satisfied with Moses' leadership and angry that they were eating manna.   They were led by a man named Korah.   This man led a revolt against the leadership, speaking to the people and telling them it was time to go back to Egypt.

Moses told them that if they were correct, then they would be leader of the band.   But if Korah and his followers were wrong, then let the earth swallow them before the eyes of all the others.   Here is the account as told by Moses.

> *Just as he finished speaking all these words, the ground beneath them split open.   The earth opened its mouth and swallowed them and their households, all Korah's people, and all [their] possessions. They went down alive into Sheol with all that belonged to them. The earth closed over them, and they vanished*

118

from the assembly. At their cries, all [the people of Israel] who were around them fled because they thought, "The earth may swallow us too!" **Numbers 16:31-34 (HCSB)**

You stretched out Your right hand, and the earth swallowed them. **Exodus 15:12 (HCSB)**

Why did God do this? God is not a god of unreasonable vengeance. Jehovah God has great love for His people. When His people are threatened by those who are trying to overthrow His plan for His people, He will protect His own.

Korah was a threat not only to God's plan, but to God's people. God will protect His people.

In this same sense, God will protect you. Walk with Him in His chosen path and lean not unto your own understanding, but only to His. Then you can rest assured that you will have the blessing of His protection against the enemies of His plan for you.

49 SPEAKING WITH DEMONS

DID YOU KNOW?

Evil spirits talked to Jesus; and Jesus spoke to them.   We are all willing to accept that Jesus dealt with the poor, the sick, the downtrodden, the crippled, and even the dead. But would a pure and righteous God want to speak to the evil dark angels of the devil?

While Jesus was teaching in His homeland, a demon-possessed man challenged Him

> *He was teaching them as one having authority. Just then a man with an unclean spirit was in their synagogue. He cried out, "What do You have to do with us, Jesus—Nazarene? Have You come to destroy us? I know who You are—the Holy One of God!"* **Mark 1:22-24 (HCSB)**

It seems that the spirits of the dark side had no trouble in recognizing the Lord.   But does that mean that God should respond?   But, of course, Jesus responds to this challenge from the Devil.

> *But Jesus rebuked him and said, "Be quiet, and come out of him!"   And the unclean spirit convulsed him, shouted with a loud voice, and came out of him. Then they were all amazed, so they began to argue*

120

*with one another, saying, "What is this? A new teaching with authority! He commands even the unclean spirits, and they obey Him." **Mark 1:25-28 (HCSB)***

Keep in mind that Jesus is Lord over ALL.   He is the King of kings and Lord of lords.   Nobody but the Father has authority over Jesus, but He has authority over all; over the good and the bad.   Jesus can order the spirits to speak, and to remain silent.

*When evening came, after the sun had set, they began bringing to Him all those who were sick and those who were demon-possessed.   The whole town was assembled at the door, and He healed many who were sick with various diseases and drove out many demons. But He would not permit the demons to speak, because they knew Him. **Mark 1:32-34 (HCSB)***

What a powerful ally we would have if only we would place ourselves in the trustworthy hands of Jesus.   He can drive out our demons, protect us from the onslaught of the devil, and heal our broken body and spirit.

Do you need this wonderful ally?   He is waiting for you to ask Him.

50 PERSONAL LOVE OF GOD

DID YOU KNOW?

God knows you.   Yes, He knows you personally. Whether or not you know Him, He knows you, and He knows all about you.   He knows your name; out of all the people in the world who have ever existed, He knows you by name.

He even calls out to people by name, and refers to others by their name. This is a personal God.

He called to Abraham to test him.

> After these things God tested Abraham and said to him, "Abraham!" "Here I am," he answered. *Genesis 22:1 (HCSB)*

And He singled out Moses while Moses was wandering in the desert.

> When the LORD saw that he had gone over to look, God called out to him from the bush, "Moses, Moses!" "Here I am," he answered. *Exodus 3:4 (HCSB)*

There are several examples of God speaking to people about other people, mentioning the others by their name. In the case of Abraham's wife, God even CHANGED her name.

122

God said to Abraham, "As for your wife Sarai, do not call her Sarai, for Sarah will be her name. **Genesis 17:15 (HCSB)**

Since He knows your name, would you suppose that He also knows your deeds and your motives?

Listen to what God said to the people of the churches of Asia Minor (Turkey).   To the church at Ephesus:

I know your works, your labor, and your endurance, and that you cannot tolerate evil. **Revelation 2:2 (HCSB)**

To the people at Smyrna:

I know your affliction and poverty, yet you are rich. **Revelation 2:9 (HCSB)**

To the church at Thyatira:

I know your works—your love, faithfulness, service, and endurance. Your last works are greater than the first. **Revelation 2:19 (HCSB)**

And the reminder that God knows, not only our works, but our reasons for doing them.

All a man's ways seem right to him, but the LORD evaluates the motives. **Proverbs 21:2 (HCSB)**

This very personal God loves you even more than He loves Himself.   He became human to die on a cruel cross for you because He loves you.   Yes, even though He knows the real you, He loves you anyway…. enough to let His own Son die in your place even while you are in rebellion against Him.

God's love was revealed among us in this way: God sent His One and Only Son into the world so that we might live through Him. Love consists in this: not that we loved God, but that He loved us and sent His Son to be the propitiation for our sins. **1 John 4:9-10 (HCSB)**

Do you know this God?   He knows you

Potholes
By Keith Rothra

Oh there won't be any potholes in those golden streets of
heaven.
There won't be any heart aches in that city, so I'm told.
The blind will see, the lame will walk.
The deaf will hear, the dumb will talk.
They'll all be praising Jesus as they walk on streets of gold.

I met a man in Arkansas, Who loved the Lord and loved the
law.
He lived what he believed from day to day.
Though ninety years had robbed his sight,
His faith was greater than his plight.
I loved the way he'd always laugh and say.

That there won't be any potholes in those golden streets of
heaven.
There won't be any heart aches in that city, so I'm told.
The blind will see, the lame will walk.
The deaf will hear, the dumb will talk.
They'll all be praising Jesus as they walk on streets of gold.

Now let me tell you now my friend, This world is coming to
an end.
The Lord is coming back to claim His bride.
Then all believing in His grace,
He's promised to prepare a place,

And in His Father's mansion we'll reside.

For there won't be any potholes in those golden streets of heaven.
There won't be any heart aches in that city, so I'm told.
The blind will see, the lame will walk.
The deaf will hear, the dumb will talk.
They'll all be praising Jesus as they walk on streets of gold.
They'll be shouting hallelujahs as they dance on streets of gold!

51   CLEANSING THE UNCLEAN

DID YOU KNOW?

There was a time when it was unlawful to touch certain people.   Not unlawful in the sense that you could be thrown in jail for it, but if you touched a person who had leprosy, you were considered "unclean" and would not be allowed around "clean" people until you had gone through a long ritual of cleansing.

The Book of Leviticus outlines the ritual laws of the Israelites.   In this book, we find these verses.

> *When the priest examines the raw flesh, he must pronounce him unclean. Raw flesh is unclean; it is a skin disease.* **Leviticus 13:15 (HCSB)**

> *Or [if] someone touches anything unclean—a carcass of an unclean wild animal, or unclean livestock, or an unclean swarming creature—without being aware of it, he is unclean and guilty.* **Leviticus 5:2 (HCSB)**

> *Whoever touches anything made unclean by a dead person or by a man who has an emission of semen, or whoever touches any swarming creature that makes him unclean or any person who makes him unclean—whatever his uncleanness— the man who touches any of these will remain unclean until evening*

and is not to eat from the holy offerings unless he has bathed his body with water. **Leviticus 22:4-6 (HCSB)**

This, however, sets the stage for a strange encounter. Jesus, God in the flesh, made a regular habit of touching people who had leprosy. Was Jesus making Himself unclean? Here is one of many New Testament examples of this.

> *While He was in one of the towns, a man was there who had a serious skin disease all over him. He saw Jesus, fell facedown, and begged Him: "Lord, if You are willing, You can make me clean." Reaching out His hand, He touched him, saying, "I am willing; be made clean," and immediately the disease left him.* **Luke 5:12-13 (HCSB)**

The dreaded disease of leprosy was considered incurable at that time. Those who contracted it were not allowed inside the city; if they did come to town, they had to cover themselves with sack cloth and ashes and holler "unclean, unclean" as they walked to warn everyone out of the way lest someone should touch them and become unclean.

Jesus was never unclean. Once the leper was touched by the healing hand of Jesus, the leper was no longer unclean either. That is the joy of the touch of God. When all the world sees you as "unclean" and otherwise a social outcast, the mere touch of Jesus can cleanse you just as Jesus did for so many lepers who believed. Just reach out and touch Him … and be clean.

52   FORGIVE THEM

DID YOU KNOW?

There were over two thousand years of prophets foretelling the coming of the great Messiah, the one who would be God in the flesh.   They came from men in Babylon, Egypt. Jerusalem, Syria, and other nations.   Prophecies came from men who did not know one another and in many cases had not read or known of the words of the others.   The men were separated not only by geographic and political boundaries, but by the impassible boundaries of centuries separating them.

In the years following, there would be a priesthood charged with the responsibility of teaching these prophecies so that the people would recognize the Messiah when He came. These men studied the good news of a coming prophet and taught their children and their successors in the priesthood. The younger generation in turn taught the great words of comfort for mankind.

And then one day, the Messiah came.   One would think that the priesthood would "crown Him with many crowns," and proclaim His appearance.   But the apostle John tells of that day:

> *He was in the world, and the world was created through Him, yet the world did not recognize Him. He*

came to His own, and His own people did not receive Him. **John 1:10-11 (HCSB)**

Although all of the prophecies were fulfilled, the priests not only didn't recognize Him, but they helped fulfill the prophecies concerning His betrayal, arrest, torture, and crucifixion.   As Jesus hung on the cross, He watched the teachers of the law as they completed the very atrocities that they had been teaching would be done.   And the scripture reveals Jesus' response to them.

> *Then Jesus said, "Father, forgive them, because they do not know what they are doing." And they divided His clothes and cast lots.* **Luke 23:34 (HCSB)**

Not aware of what they were doing, they destroyed the One who had come to save them.

It is written that He will come back again.   Will you recognize Him when He comes, or will He again say those brokenhearted words?   "Father, forgive them for they know not what they are doing."

He is coming again, but those who don't know Him will not go with Him.   He won't have any trouble recognizing you. Will you know Him?

53   ARE YOU READY?

DID YOU KNOW?

The end times are near… or maybe they're not.   It seems like every other day I have someone asking me if I see the end times approaching.   Then they want to know my opinion.

I have read the scriptures from the Old Testament prophets, and some of their words are tantalizing, but not certain for any conclusions.

Our Lord Jesus gave us some good insight in Matthew 24. We should not listen to anyone who tells us that the Lord has returned… that He is out in the desert.   When He comes, He will come in the clouds.

Paul told the people in Thessalonica this word:

> *About the times and the seasons: Brothers, you do not need anything to be written to you. For you yourselves know very well that the Day of the Lord will come just like a thief in the night.* ***1 Thessalonians 5:1-2 (HCSB)***

Jesus said that no one will know the day or the hour, but only the Father Himself.   When He comes, it will be like the rains of Noah's ark.   Noah's neighbors probably chided him terribly for his silliness.   Why would you need a boat in

THIS area?   There has never been a flood … anywhere. We are safe!

> *When they say, "Peace and security," then sudden destruction comes on them, like labor pains come on a pregnant woman, and they will not escape.* **1 Thessalonians 5:3 (HCSB)**

We need to be aware of the fact that Jesus is coming back. When He is coming is not relevant; what is relevant is the fact that He will return.   Being aware of that fact, we should walk in that light of wisdom … and share it with others.

> *But you, brothers, are not in the dark, for this day to overtake you like a thief.   For you are all sons of light and sons of the day. We do not belong to the night or the darkness.* **1 Thessalonians 5:4-5 (HCSB)**

God does not call us to darkness, nor to ignorance.   He has told us that He is coming back for us.   The "when" is not the question; but the real question is this: "Are you ready?"

Walk in wisdom.   Walk in the light.   Walk in faith.   Then, WHEN He returns, you will be ready.

54   WEALTH AND JOY

DID YOU KNOW?

I been blessed with luxury, and I have been blessed with poverty.   At one point I lived in a 19-room mansion overlooking Lake Erie.   It was not a time that I would consider as happy.   I lived 14 years in what some called "the little red shack in the swamp" where our family, through sickness and in health, had love and joy … it was a great place for my childhood.

I know very wealthy people who are miserable.   I know poor people who are miserable too, but some others are very happy, even joyful, in their poverty.   Wealth does not come from money; true wealth is a condition of the heart.

King Solomon was the wealthiest man in the world.   Just the provisions for the daily feasts at his table would astound most people.   Here is the daily grocery list for Solomon's house.

> *Solomon's provisions for one day were 150 bushels of fine flour and 300 bushels of meal, 10 fattened oxen, 20 range oxen, and 100 sheep, besides deer, gazelles, roebucks, and pen-fed poultry…(and more).* **1 Kings 4:22-23 (HCSB)**

Compare this with his father's diet when on the run from King Saul.   David had to sneak into the temple and steal the showbread that was reserved for the priests, because he had nothing to eat.   Yet, one generation later, his son is wallowing in luxury.

Was Solomon happy with all of his gold, silver, land, herds, and servants?   Listen to his opinion of it all.

> *I built houses and planted vineyards for myself. I made gardens and parks for myself and planted every kind of fruit tree in them.   I constructed reservoirs of water for myself from which to irrigate a grove of flourishing trees. I acquired male and female servants and had slaves who were born in my house. I also owned many herds of cattle and flocks, more than all who were before me in Jerusalem.   I also amassed silver and gold for myself, and the treasure of kings and provinces. I gathered male and female singers for myself, and many concubines, the delights of men. …. All that my eyes desired, I did not deny them. I did not refuse myself any pleasure, for I took pleasure in all my struggles. This was my reward for all my struggles. When I considered all that I had accomplished and what I had labored to achieve, I found everything to be futile and a pursuit of the wind. There was nothing to be gained under the sun.* **Ecclesiastes 2:4-9, 10-11 (HCSB)**

Jesus told us the source of joy.   It was not things.

> *But seek first the kingdom of God and His righteousness, and all these things will be provided for you.* **Matthew 6:33 (HCSB)**

55   SCORPION HORSES

DID YOU KNOW?

The locust is a dangerous threat to the farmer.   A single swarm of locusts has been known to totally wipe out the grain crop of a whole nation.   They eat everything in their way, from crops to trees, bark and all, and vineyards, and even grain stored in silos.   They are basically grasshoppers and are a rather ugly sort of insect.

But there is a swarm of locusts coming that will not only eat the crops, but they will attack people and sting them with the sting of a scorpion.   And they won't look like grasshoppers; they will look like horses, but have faces like men.   These little flying man/horses with scorpion stingers will make people miserable with their bite.   They will be sent by the Lord to menace those people who have not accepted Christ as Lord.   John describes them this way.

> *The appearance of the locusts was like horses equipped for battle. Something like gold crowns was on their heads; their faces were like men's faces;* ***Revelation 9:7 (HCSB)***

Initially, they have the power of mere locusts, but then it all changes.

Then locusts came out of the smoke on to the earth, and power was given to them like the power that scorpions have on the earth. **Revelation 9:3 (HCSB)**

But then God directed them to not act like locusts.   The crops were safe; the trees were untouched; the storehouses were unmolested.

They were told not to harm the grass of the earth, or any green plant, or any tree, but only people who do not have God's seal on their foreheads. They were not permitted to kill them but were to torment [them] for five months; their torment is like the torment caused by a scorpion when it strikes a man. **Revelation 9:4-5 (HCSB)**

These little critters will harass the non-believers, but they cannot kill them.   The victims will not die, but they will wish they could because of their misery.

In those days people will seek death and will not find it; they will long to die, but death will flee from them. **Revelation 9: 6 (HCSB)**

A key to this is found in verse four.   They were to attack only people who do not have God's seal on their foreheads.
The Christians will be free from these attackers.   Why?
God will take care of His own, just as He promises.   He takes care of His own even today.   Are you one of His?
Whose side do you want to be on?

56   AVOID DECEIVERS

DID YOU KNOW?

I am saddened every time I read about another cult leader who takes his/her people off on some tangent away from the teaching of the true Gospel.   There have been some really tragic disasters in the past; the Jonestown mass suicide/murders being among the most horrible.

But the leaders are not always an obvious charlatan or mass murderer.   Usually the leader is a well-spoken, highly-charismatic person who elicits the love and discipleship necessary through tender words and promises of unending love.

Let me see if I can make this obvious.   If someone promised you that they were going to lead you into poverty, pain, and physical torment, who in their right mind would follow him?   But the sweeter promises coupled with philosophical pictures of utopia have a much greater appeal.

But here is the warning offered by the Apostle Paul:

> *Be careful that no one takes you captive through philosophy and empty deceit based on human tradition, based on the elemental forces of the world, and not based on Christ.* **Colossians 2:8 (HCSB)**

If anyone teaches a doctrine of eternal life to be attained through anything other than the grace of God, freely given through the death and resurrection of Jesus Christ …. do not believe them. They are false teachers.

> I am saying this so that no one will deceive you with persuasive arguments. **Colossians 2:4 (HCSB)**

I uphold Paul's caution with these words from the Apostle John:

> Many deceivers have gone out into the world; they do not confess the coming of Jesus Christ in the flesh. This is the deceiver and the antichrist. Watch yourselves so you don't lose what we have worked for, but that you may receive a full reward. Anyone who does not remain in Christ's teaching but goes beyond it, does not have God. The one who remains in that teaching, this one has both the Father and the Son. If anyone comes to you and does not bring this teaching, do not receive him into your home, and don't say, "Welcome," to him; for the one who says, "Welcome," to him shares in his evil works. **2 John 1:7-11 (HCSB)**

57   QUANTUM LEAP

DID YOU KNOW?

There used to be a television show called Quantum Leap.
Maybe you remember it.   The main character would find
himself suddenly projected into some oddball period of
history for which he was always unprepared to understand.
Just about the time that he got adjusted to his new
surroundings, he got zapped out of it and into another one.

Can you imagine living in one period of history and suddenly
being thrust into a totally different century?   That's great
stuff for science fiction.   The program lasted a few seasons
and had reasonable success, in part, because it was purely
sci-fi in its style.

There was a man named John who was sitting on a Greek
island about ninety years after the birth of Jesus.   He was
elderly, and yet was a threat to the local governors in what is
now western Turkey, so he was exiled to the barren Island of
Patmos.

While on the island, John was praying in the Spirit, and was
taken up by God to a place where he served as a witness to
what would be in our future.

> *After this I looked, and there in heaven was an open
> door. The first voice that I had heard speaking to me*

139

*like a trumpet said, "Come up here, and I will show you what must take place after this." **Revelation 4:1 (HCSB)***

That's right, a man who was living two thousand years ago was Quantum Leaped into our future.   Then he was told to write down everything that he saw so that we could read about our future from someone who witnessed it 2000 years ago.

No matter how I look at this, it makes no sense to me… until I consider that to the Lord a day is but a thousand years and a thousand years is but a day.   God is not restrained by the shackles of time.   When He said let there be light, He already knew about your birth, your life, your joys, and your sin … and, yes, even your mortal death.

Because God knew our future before we were even born, why could He not easily show the future to a man named John and tell him to write it down?

If you read the Revelation, which is John's record of what he saw, you will find that God has special rewards for those who invest their faith in Him, but terrible consequences for those who will not.   In order to redeem that promise, you must give your faith and trust to Jesus Christ.

Are you ready to experience the Quantum Leap?

58   DO YOU LOVE ME?

DID YOU KNOW?

I love my Lord and Savior, Jesus of Nazareth.   The question that He asks of me is, "How much?"   He also asks me, "How do you love me?"   Is He my friend?   Is He my lover?   Is He my inseparable companion that could never lose my love?

The Greek language, in which the New Testament is written, has different forms of the word "love."   There is a romantic love that is "*eros*" love.   This is the love that I have for my wife; but I also have a different love for my wife and friend. I love her with a love that the Greeks call "*phileo*."   It is a brotherly love.

But the third kind of love is the love that God has for us, and wants us to have for one another; it is "*agapao*."   Most people call it "agape" (pronounced *ah GAH' peh*) love and it is a love that has no limit.   It is a love that loves you no matter what.

When Jesus was sitting with Peter on the seashore, He asked Peter about his love.

> *When they had eaten breakfast, Jesus asked Simon Peter, "Simon, son of John, do you love Me more than these?" "Yes, Lord," he said to Him, "You know that I*

love You." "Feed My lambs," He told him. A second time He asked him, "Simon, son of John, do you love Me?" "Yes, Lord," he said to Him, "You know that I love You." "Shepherd My sheep," He told him. He asked him the third time, "Simon, son of John, do you love Me?" Peter was grieved that He asked him the third time, "Do you love Me?" He said, "Lord, You know everything! You know that I love You." "Feed My sheep," Jesus said. **John 21:15-17 (HCSB)**

Many teachers say that Peter was upset because Jesus asked him the same question three times. Not so if you read it in Greek.

Peter, do you agapao me? Peter responded with, Yes Lord, I phileo you.

Do you love me without end? Peter responds with essentially, "Yes, we are friends."

They exchanged this same dialogue again, with the response that "I love you with phileo love."

Then Jesus turned it around by asking Peter, "Do you phileo me?" Basically, "Are we friends?" And Peter was upset because Jesus asked him that.

The question is still there. How do you love Jesus? He is the lover of your soul. He is your best friend. And He should be the one you love with an unchangeable, unbreakable love called (in Greek) agapao.

Do you love Jesus? HOW do you love Jesus?

59 BREPHOS – A CHILD

DID YOU KNOW?

The Greek word for child is **BREPHOS**
   It was used for JOHN the Baptist … when he was in the womb_of Elizabeth.
   It was used for JESUS ….. in the manger.
   It was used for TIMOTHY …. as he learned scriptures as a young boy.

The THAYER GREEK LEXICON defines "BREPHOS" as an
   "embryo, fetus, newborn child, young child, or nursing child."

So the Bible CLEARLY makes the UNBORN equal to the BORN child.

There are some who profess that life does not begin until the time that a child draws the first breath after birth.   This is not the case.

When did you or I begin?   The Bible tells us.

> *Coastlands, listen to me; distant peoples, pay attention. The LORD called me before I was born. He named me while I was in my mother's womb.* **Isaiah 49:1 (HCSB)**

143

Every person is a creation of God. The oldest person was made by God, but so was the youngest; even the child who is yet unborn is a creation of God.

> *The Spirit of God has made me, and the breath of the Almighty gives me life.* **Job 33:4 (HCSB)**

Here is an expression of this from King David.

> *I will praise You because I have been remarkably and wonderfully made. Your works are wonderful, and I know [this] very well. My bones were not hidden from You when I was made in secret, when I was formed in the depths of the earth. Your eyes saw me when I was formless; all [my] days were written in Your book and planned before a single one of them began.* **Psalm 139:14-16 (HCSB)**

A baby in the womb is not a part of the mother's body. Yet there are those who claim a right to destroy an unborn child because the mother has the right to choose everything about her body.

> *Don't you know that your body is a sanctuary of the Holy Spirit who is in you, whom you have from God? You are not your own,* **1 Corinthians 6:19 (HCSB)**

God creates life; only God creates life. What God has brought together let no one put asunder.

Please pray for mothers who might be considering terminating their pregnancy through abortion. Pray that the child will become what God intended it to be.

144

Please pray for mothers who have made the decision to abort. They have made a painful decision. Ask God to place His arms around them and give them peace. While you're at it, your arms around them would help too.

60   TELLING OTHERS

DID YOU KNOW?

Good news travels fast.   There was a gas station in Prattville, Alabama, that opened with a bang.   They offered gas at more than a dollar per gallon below the other stations. The place was a madhouse.   Cars were backed up for blocks.   He thought he would make it through the first day but had to bring in tankers twice for that first day to keep up with the demand.

The station got a lot of attention, and after that grand opening, people kept coming back even after the prices went up to the rest of the market.   People figured out that they could get a good deal at this place and they liked what they found.   Then they told their friends; and when the friends found out that it was a good deal, they told more friends.

This same thing is true when sharing your faith.   Here is how one of the first converts to Christ responded to his new faith.

> *Andrew, Simon Peter's brother, was one of the two who heard John and followed Him.   He first found his own brother Simon and told him, "We have found the Messiah!" (which means "Anointed One"), and he brought Simon to Jesus. **John 1:40-42 (HCSB)***

I have never met anyone who regretted accepting salvation in Jesus Christ. They have all been glad that someone told them about this "good deal." As a matter of fact, most go out and tell their friends who don't know about it. Some of those friends will come and check it out and then go tell others.

There was the woman at the well in Samaria who ran into town and told everyone to come and see the Messiah. They came and saw … and they believed. Many came to know about Jesus through that encounter with that one woman.

Jesus had the same idea. He told us to tell people about the Gospel message wherever we go. The Apostle Paul gave the same idea when he urged Timothy, disciple preacher, to do this:

> *And what you have heard from me in the presence of many witnesses, commit to faithful men who will be able to teach others also.* **2 Timothy 2:2 (HCSB)**

Who have you told about Jesus this week?

Thank You, Lord
By Keith Rothra

I just want to thank you, Lord,
For what you've done in my life.
I just want to thank you, Lord,
For saving me from all of that strife.
So every morning of every day,
I'll get down on my knees and pray and say
I just want to thank you, Lord,
For what you've done in my life.

I just want to thank you, Lord,
For what you've done in my life.
I just want to thank you, Lord,
For teaching me wrong from right.
So every morning of every day,
I'll get down on my knees and pray and say
I just want to thank you, Lord,
For what you've done in my life.

61   HEALING

DID YOU KNOW?

I once met a man who asked me and my friends to pray for his family.   He said that they didn't know the Lord, and that he hoped that somehow they would be led to Him.   I don't think he knew what he was asking for, but he got the answer to his prayer, exactly in the form he expressed it.

One morning I was at a day surgery center with my wife for some minor surgery.   (Because it was on her, I can call it minor. Any surgery on me, even a tooth extraction, is a big deal.)   While she was in having her procedure done, I saw this friend.   I asked what brought him there and he said that his father was bleeding at the base of his esophagus.   They had stopped the bleeding once, but it started again and the doctor said it was too late.   It was just a matter of time before he bled out.

I asked where his family was; he led me to them in a separate room.   I told them that God does His best work when the doctors have said that there is no hope.   I asked if they would pray with me, and they agreed.   I prayed that God would help this family through saving their father, and that the family could see the power of God and come to believe.

About twenty minutes later a befuddled doctor came out and told the family that somehow the bleeding just stopped. He had no explanation, but said that the man would be ok.

At this point the friend pointed at me and said, "He did it!" I was shocked.

I told them that NO, I didn't do it, but that I did nothing more than they themselves could have done if they would put their faith in God. I asked God in the name of Jesus and God answered so that they might have faith.

In the same manner, Peter was criminally charged for healing a man, and he replied this way:

> If we are being examined today about a good deed done to a disabled man—by what means he was healed— [10] let it be known to all of you and to all the people of Israel, that by the name of Jesus Christ the Nazarene—whom you crucified and whom God raised from the dead—by Him this man is standing here before you healthy. **Acts 4:9-10 (HCSB)**

God will heal according to His will, but He wants us to ask. Here is His promise through James, the brother of Jesus:

> Is anyone among you sick? He should call for the elders of the church, and they should pray over him after anointing him with olive oil in the name of the Lord. [15] The prayer of faith will save the sick person, and the Lord will restore him to health; if he has committed sins, he will be forgiven. **James 5:14-15 (HCSB)**

Only believe and step boldly forward.

62   LAODICEA

DID YOU KNOW?

God loves you and wants you to trust Him for all your needs. When you turn away from Him because you think you can handle all your own needs by yourself, you place yourself in grave danger.   When a person thinks that they do not need God, they are prime pickings for the devil.

> *So, whoever thinks he stands must be careful not to fall.* ***1 Corinthians 10:12 (HCSB)***

He sent a message to the people of Laodicea, a church that was extremely rich and had come to the opinion that they could take care of themselves.   The Lord's message was not very comforting to them.

> *Because you say, 'I'm rich; I have become wealthy and need nothing,' and you don't know that you are wretched, pitiful, poor, blind, and naked, I advise you to buy from Me gold refined in the fire so that you may be rich, white clothes so that you may be dressed and your shameful nakedness not be exposed, and ointment to spread on your eyes so that you may see.* ***Revelation 3:17-18 (HCSB)***

God's thoughts toward Laodicea were much the same as His message to the Romans who had forgotten Him.

151

For though they knew God, they did not glorify Him as God or show gratitude. Instead, their thinking became nonsense, and their senseless minds were darkened. **Romans 1:21 (HCSB)**

God is the provider of all things.   Often today it is easy for us to forget that except for the grace and provision of God, we would have nothing.   He told the people of Laodicea His opinion of them.

I know your works, that you are neither cold nor hot. I wish that you were cold or hot.   So, because you are lukewarm, and neither hot nor cold, I am going to vomit you out of My mouth. **Revelation 3:15-16 (HCSB)**

God still loved the people of Rome and of Laodicea, just as He loves us, even when we forget who got us where we are. He had such strong words for them because He loved them.

As many as I love, I rebuke and discipline. So be committed and repent. **Revelation 3:19 (HCSB)**

63   FALSE TEACHERS

DID YOU KNOW?

There are many roads that will take you to Rome.   This simple statement has been used for centuries to explain that there is more than one way to draw a conclusion or get to a particular destination.   I have even heard this offered to me to tell me that there is more than one way to get to Heaven.

It is true that there are many roads leading to Rome; I have been there and got lost, but kept following signs that led me back to the center of town.   However, there is only one road that leads to Heaven, all others lead to eternal destruction.

> *"Enter through the narrow gate. For the gate is wide and the road is broad that leads to destruction, and there are many who go through it.   **Matthew 7:13 (HCSB)***

The only true way to Heaven was told to us by our Messiah, Jesus.

> *Jesus told him, "I am the way, the truth, and the life. No one comes to the Father except through Me. **John 14:6 (HCSB)***

People may come to your door and tell you that you can earn your way to heaven through your own hard work; do not believe them.

Some may promise you that a new messiah has come and he will lead you to eternal happiness; again, do not believe them.

When you feel a spiritual presence that leads you to seek a new way to salvation, pray to God to rebuke that spirit, it is not of God.

When anyone tells you that there is a newer prophet of God who brings a new set of rules; they are liars and the truth is not in them.

The Apostle Paul cautioned the people of Galatia against these false teachers.   We need to listen to his message.

> *I am amazed that you are so quickly turning away from Him who called you by the grace of Christ /and are turning/ to a different gospel—   not that there is another /gospel/, but there are some who are troubling you and want to change the good news about the Messiah. But even if we or an angel from heaven should preach to you a gospel other than what we have preached to you, a curse be on him! As we have said before, I now say again: If anyone preaches to you a gospel contrary to what you received, a curse be on him!* **Galatians 1:6-9 (HCSB)**

Amen.

64   14 BILLION MANSIONS

DID YOU KNOW?

Jesus told us that He was going to His Father's house and He was going to prepare a place for us.   He said:

> "Your heart must not be troubled. Believe in God; believe also in Me.   In My Father's house are many dwelling places; if not, I would have told you. I am going away to prepare a place for you. **John 14:1-2 (HCSB)**

In the history of the earth, there have been roughly 14 Billion people.   Of those, a little over half of them are alive today. Will there be room enough for all those people in that eternal city that God has prepared for us?

Is it possible that God has prepared a place for every person who was ever born?   Only God knows how many of the 14 Billion will actually be in heaven, but we are assured that some will not make it.   But how much space will there be in that city?

Here is the size of the city:

> The city is laid out in a square; its length and width are the same. He measured the city with the rod at 12,000 stadia. Its length, width, and height are equal. **Revelation 21:16 (HCSB)**

Twelve thousand stadia is equal to roughly 1400 miles. Therefore, the city will be 1400 miles long, wide, and high. If you would care to do the math for this, you will find that this "city" contains 2,744,000,000 cubic miles.   If the height of each person's "mansion" was limited to a square mile that is 1000 feet high, there will be nearly 14 Billion square miles available, one square mile for every person ever born in the history of Earth, with each having a 1000 foot high ceiling.

If half of the people who ever existed were allowed into heaven, and scripture implies there will be less than that, then there is ample room for you to have your own golf course, (strange priorities) or just about anything else you would want to establish.

But you would probably be joining the everlasting chorus at the foot of His throne, and, surely, nobody would want to play golf when they can be in the presence of God.   Maybe I'll have a nine iron in my hand at the throne?

Just rest assured that Jesus HAS prepared a place for you.

65   SEEK TO BE A SERVANT

DID YOU KNOW?

He who blows his own horn is not welcome in the band. When a band plays a piece, every player has to follow the same sheet of music.   One who plays to his own music will make the rest of the band look bad and infuriate them all.

In a band or orchestra, there is a system of ranking the players.   The best violinist is seated in the "first chair." The others are ranked lower.   While most would like to be considered as "first chair," it would be a foolish move to walk in and just assume your right to sit there.   Only the leader can decide who will take the best seat.

This is not a new concept.   Jesus ran into this with His disciples.

> Then James and John, the sons of Zebedee, approached Him and said, "Teacher, we want You to do something for us if we ask You."   "What do you want Me to do for you?" He asked them. They answered Him, "Allow us to sit at Your right and at Your left in Your glory." **Mark 10:35-37 (HCSB)**

They went to the "band leader" and asked for "first chair." As with the band or orchestra, the other members were upset with their "blowing their own horn." It can be embarrassing to sit in the first chair and be asked to move down a few seats. It would be far better to sit in the fourth chair and be asked to move up toward the first.

Seeking the seat of honor is selfish. There is no room for selfishness in a Christian life.

> *Jesus called them over and said to them, "You know that those who are regarded as rulers of the Gentiles dominate them, and their men of high positions exercise power over them. But it must not be like that among you. On the contrary, whoever wants to become great among you must be your servant, and whoever wants to be first among you must be a slave to all. For even the Son of Man did not come to be served, but to serve, and to give His life—a ransom for many."* **Mark 10:42-45 (HCSB)**

Seek to be a servant of all and you will find yourself elevated by those around you. Seek to be elevated and …. well …. you know. The elevator goes both ways. Go out and elevate others.

66   SPEAKING CHRISTIANESE

DID YOU KNOW?

We don't always say what we mean … or what we mean to convey.

Someone told me about a new HMO that opened in an old building.   A man came in and told the receptionist that he had shingles.   She handed him a clipboard full of forms and asked him to fill them out.

He began but he came back up to the desk.   The lady asked, "what can I do for you today?"   He said again …. " have shingles."   She told him to be seated and they would get to him soon.   After about twenty minutes he returned to the desk and said, "Ma'am, I have shingles here …" and she interrupted with "can you tell me where you have shingles?" He said, "on my truck in the parking lot.   Where do you want them loaded?"

We do the same thing by talking Christianese.   We know what we are talking about, but others haven't a clue.   I was thirty-seven years old before I knew what it meant to be "born again."   It's no wonder that Nicodemus was dumbfounded by that statement by Jesus.

We sing songs like "there is a fountain filled with blood", and then we ask in song, "Are You Washed in the Blood?" Do people outside the church have ANY idea what we are talking about?

When Jesus told the people that they needed to eat His flesh and drink His blood, many turned away from Him that day.

> *The one who eats My flesh and drinks My blood lives in Me, and I in him. … From that moment many of His disciples turned back and no longer accompanied Him.* **John 6:56, 66 (HCSB)**

They didn't understand the truth He was trying to give them. Today Christians across the world take the Holy Communion as sharing in the flesh and blood of Christ. But the non-believing world has no idea what we are doing or why.

We face a general population who does not share our vocabulary of Christianese, but we use words like "saved" and "born again" when we try to tell them about Jesus. Thirty years ago, this language scared me away from "church people." They were weird! (Now I am weird!)

Perhaps we could do a better job of winning people to the Kingdom (that's one of those words) if we choose our words from the bottom shelf of vocabulary instead of from the heavenly realms. Let's just share what Jesus has done for us personally. I am sure it can be done with a limited amount of Christianese.

67 GREATER LOVE HAS NO MAN

DID YOU KNOW?

There is no national military in the world that has children running to them instead of away from them … except the US military.   In spite of accusations by misinformed politicians who have ulterior motivations for their rant, the American military is not a murderous gang of child molesters.   They give candy, food, medical attention and water to starving children and families all across the world.

There has been no nation in the world that has been as generous as America with its material wealth by giving it to the needy throughout the world.   Even our enemies see our people showing up in times of calamity such as earthquakes or tidal waves … and yes, destruction brought against them by other nations.

There is also no nation in the world that has been so generous with the blood of their own sons and daughters; blood spilt to buy freedom for people that we don't even know, but who deserve the same liberties that we enjoy in our land.

> *For rarely will someone die for a just person—though for a good person perhaps someone might even dare to die.* ***Romans 5:7 (HCSB)***

How do you thank a person who has placed their own life in jeopardy in order to ensure that yours will be free?   I had a friend in Jamestown NY whose name is on a very lonely wall in the Washington DC Capitol Mall, because he laid down his life for people he didn't know.   I know people whose body has been broken because they put themselves in harm's way to give others freedom.   I know men and women whose emotional stability will always be impaired because of the things they saw and did to secure someone else's liberty.

In Europe, there are several cemeteries, one holding my uncle, Virgil Rothra.   Each holds the remains of thousands of Americans who went there to liberate those countries from the Nazi atrocities.   There is one in the Philippines that holds over 30,000 Americans.

How do we thank these brave souls?   There are not adequate words to express what they deserve.   Other than this:

> "*No one has greater love than this, that someone would lay down his life for his friends*".... **John 15:13 (HCSB)**   ··· Or for people they don't even know.

Do you enjoy your freedom?   First, thank God.   Thank Him for the brave men and women who stepped forward to defend what God has given us.   Then, find a veteran and thank him/her for such selflessness.

Keith A. Rothra, Major, USAF, Retired

… and all my veteran brothers and sisters.

68   OUT ON A LIMB FOR JESUS

DID YOU KNOW?

Do you remember this song? .... "Zacchaeus was a wee little man; a wee little man was he."

Most children who have ever attended a vacation Bible school sang that song.   It was usually followed by the story of this man who I always imagined as being about four feet short or less ... a dwarf perhaps.

Do you remember going to parades as a kid?   There was always a bunch of big people standing on the curb, and being a little kid ... about two feet less in altitude ... I couldn't see the parade.   One time a few kids climbed on top of the Post Office building to watch, and were severely chewed out for their disrespectful behavior.   They were chewed out by the same people who wouldn't let them in front of them at the curb.   These kids just found a solution to their problem ... they wanted to see the parade.

This was Zacchaeus' problem.   It wasn't actually a parade coming by, but it was Jesus and His followers.   With all those "regular' people standing at the roadside, short little Zacchaeus had to take drastic measures.   He couldn't climb on top of the Post Office … they didn't have one … so he climbed a tree.

> *There was a man named Zacchaeus who was a chief tax collector, and he was rich. He was trying to see who Jesus was, but he was not able because of the crowd, since he was a short man. So running ahead, he climbed up a sycamore tree to see Jesus, since He was about to pass that way.* **Luke 19:2-4 (HCSB)**

Zacchaeus was considered a sinner by most Jews. He was not only a tax collector, he was a chief tax collector; he was hated all the more for "stealing" from his own people. He wanted to be free from his burden; he wanted to be free from his sin. He knew the only way was Jesus… So Zacchaeus went out on a limb.

Jesus recognized Zacchaeus, saw his faith, and rewarded him. He went to his house for dinner and forgave his sin … because Zacchaeus was willing to go out on a limb for Jesus.

Want freedom from your current situation? Need help? Go out on a limb and call on Jesus. He will come to your house, too. Then all your past will be gone. Freedom by going out on a limb! It's your turn.

69   OVER-RATING MYSELF

DID YOU KNOW?

When I was in the Air Force, I was incredible!   Everything I did was wonderful, and I was capable of singlehandedly saving the whole world.   I have proof of this.   I still have all of my Officer Effectiveness Reports (OERs).   These are the performance reports that are required of every USAF officer each year, and for lieutenants, twice per year.   These reports described the phenomenal feats that I accomplished; each one making me far above all of my peers.   I was wonderful.

Now let's tell the rest of the story.   I wrote those evaluations.   That's right, I wrote most of my own evaluations, and then my supervisor signed them.   Since these are the documents that they use to determine who gets promoted … or passed over for promotion …. I wanted them to describe an officer of incredible talents and abilities. They said just that.   What does truth have to do with it?

I was not a born-again Christian in those days and did not know what the Bible's Holy scripture tell us about such a thing.

For if anyone considers himself to be something when he is nothing, he deceives himself. But each person should examine his own work, and then he will have a reason for boasting in himself alone, and not in respect to someone else. For each person will have to carry his own load. **Galatians 6:3-5 (HCSB)**

All that we are is what God has made us. We have no reason to boast about anything of our own, because none of it was of our making. Our salvation came about not because we chose God, but because God chose us. We put our faith in Christ after God gave us the faith to invest … it wasn't our own. Pastors should only be pastors because God called them, not because they sought the glory of a pulpit. The same can be said of a deacon, Sunday school teacher, or choir member. All that we are is what God has made us… nothing more.

But as for me, I will never boast about anything except the cross of our Lord Jesus Christ. The world has been crucified to me through the cross, and I to the world. **Galatians 6:14 (HCSB)**

Let us each walk in humility, considering others above ourselves, and ourselves to be servants unto them.

And whoever welcomes Me welcomes Him who sent Me. For whoever is least among you—this one is great." **Luke 9:48B (HCSB)**

70   JOSIAH – THE GOOD KING

DID YOU KNOW?

You are not defined by your parents or your childhood circumstances.   You are defined by your relationship with your Lord and God.

Take, for example three generations defined in 2 Kings 21 – 22.   Manasseh was an evil king.   He worshipped false gods and led his people of Judah to do the same.

Manasseh's son, Amon, followed the leadership of his father and was as evil as Manasseh.

Does this mean that the next generation will do the same? No!   Josiah followed the ways of David and worshipped God.

> *Amon was 22 years old when he became king and reigned two years in Jerusalem. His mother's name was Meshullemeth daughter of Haruz; [she was] from Jotbah. He did what was evil in the LORD's sight as his father Manasseh had done. He walked in all the ways his father had walked; he served the idols his father had served, and he worshiped them. He abandoned the LORD God of his ancestors and did not walk in the way of the LORD.* ***2 Kings 21:19-22 (HCSB)***

Amon's servants conspired against the king and killed him in his own house. Then the common people executed all those who had conspired against King Amon and made his son Josiah king in his place. **2 Kings 21:23-24 (HCSB)**

Josiah was eight years old when he became king and reigned 31 years in Jerusalem. ... He did what was right in the LORD's sight and walked in all the ways of his ancestor David; he did not turn to the right or the left. **2 Kings 22:1-2 (HCSB)**

Some today blame their bad behavior on their parents or their poor upbringing. Others have thrived in spite of their meager childhood.

We should all lean on our Heavenly Father rather than our earthly one. Our obligation is to live in a way that will bring honor to our earthly father through our gratitude and obedience to our Holy Father.

Jesus Died for Me
By Keith Rothra

Would you send your son out to suffer in torture?
Would you send him out to be nailed to a tree?
Would you let him go if you knew this would happen?
Well, that's what my Lord did, and He did it for me.

Jesus died for me,
Up there on Calvary.
He died so that I could know life eternal.
He died for sinners like me.

When Jesus was born, all the heavens proclaimed Him.
The angels sent shepherds and wise men to see.
But up on that cross was a much greater victory,
When He bought salvation for you and for me.

Jesus died for me,
Up there on Calvary.
He died so that I could know life eternal.
He died for sinners like me.
He died for you and for me.

71 ONE TRUTH

DID YOU KNOW?

We should all know that God loved us so much that He gave His only begotten Son so that whoever would believe in Him would not perish, but have everlasting life.   That simple, yet profound, statement is not only the most famous of all scripture verses, but is actually the Gospel in one verse.   It is the very truth of the purpose of God, and is the ONLY truth by which we are saved; for there can be but one truth.

Some preach what they call another truth; a message of another prophet or another savior.   They are false teachers, yet some who have ventured near to Jesus have turned away to follow their false teaching.   This is not a new thing; it has been happening for two thousand years.   Paul wrote of it to the people at Galatia.

> *I am amazed that you are so quickly turning away from Him who called you by the grace of Christ /and are turning/ to a different gospel—   not that there is another /gospel/, but there are some who are troubling you and want to change the good news about the Messiah.   **Galatians 1:6-7 (HCSB)***

People knock on my door from time to time teaching strange concepts about my Lord Jesus.   Some say I could also be a god (which I know is a blasphemous lie); others tell me that

Jesus is an archangel (which is also a lie).   Then others teach that a new messiah has come with a whole new road to salvation… even Jesus warned us about that lie.

Paul continued with his warning to the Galatians this way.

But even if we or an angel from heaven should preach to you a gospel other than what we have preached to you, a curse be on him! As we have said before, I now say again: If anyone preaches to you a gospel contrary to what you received, a curse be on him!
Galatians 1:8-9 (HCSB)

Stand on the truth .. for there is only One who is the truth.

Jesus told him, "I am the way, the truth, and the life. No one comes to the Father except through Me.
John 14:6 (HCSB)

72   FOUNDATION OF SAND

DID YOU KNOW?

My neighbor was unhappy with me.   His house was trying to fall down, and he said it was my fault.   His slab foundation was cracking and the house was sinking on that corner.   The reason for the crack and the settling, he was told, was a sweet gum tree which was in my yard.   The tree's roots had reached underground into his yard and under his house.   The roots loosened the soil under the foundation and his house was sinking into the hole.

We need to be careful when we build something; be sure that the foundation is solid, and that nothing can undermine it.   Jesus pointed to that fact when He was describing faith.

> *But everyone who hears these words of Mine and doesn't act on them will be like a foolish man who built his house on the sand.   The rain fell, the rivers rose, the winds blew and pounded that house, and it collapsed. And its collapse was great!"* **Matthew 7:26-27 (HCSB)**

But my neighbor recognized his problem.   I cut the evil tree down and poisoned the root system.   He called on the people who could fix the foundation.   The problem has been solved.

I had a different problem; maybe you had this problem too. It wasn't my house that was built on a bad foundation, it was my faith.   I relied upon myself and the fact that I was a "good person" as the basis that God would allow me into His heaven.   That, my friend, is a very bad foundation.   You need to start any foundation with a cornerstone, and the only acceptable cornerstone of faith is Jesus Christ.   With that anchor in place, the foundation of real faith was laid.

Jesus told us about that, too.

> *"Therefore, everyone who hears these words of Mine and acts on them will be like a sensible man who built his house on the rock.   The rain fell, the rivers rose, and the winds blew and pounded that house. Yet it didn't collapse, because its foundation was on the rock. **Matthew 7:24-25 (HCSB)***

What is your spiritual house built upon?   Are you allowing your friends and neighbors to undermine the foundation of your faith? …. Or is it based on the unshakable cornerstone of Christ?

73   DINING WITH JESUS

DID YOU KNOW?

Ghosts don't eat.   They have no need for food.   Spirits don't eat … for the same reason.   But When Jesus appeared to the apostles on the night of His resurrection, they were having trouble believing their eyes.   They thought they were being visited by a ghost, or spirit.

> *But they were startled and terrified and thought they were seeing a ghost.* **Luke 24:37 (HCSB)**

But Jesus knows what the men are thinking.   He invited them to look at His hands and feet to prove who He was.

> *"Why are you troubled?" He asked them. "And why do doubts arise in your hearts?   Look at My hands and My feet, that it is I Myself! Touch Me and see, because a ghost does not have flesh and bones as you can see I have." **Luke 24:38-39 (HCSB)***

But that didn't solve the problem for them of whether or not He was a ghost.   So here is how Luke recorded the testimony of those present.

> *But while they still were amazed and unbelieving because of [their] joy, He asked them, "Do you have anything here to eat?"   So they gave Him a piece of*

a broiled fish, and He took it and ate in their presence.
Luke 24:41-43 (HCSB)

A few weeks after this incident, Jesus calls to Peter and John and others from the shoreline to bring their boats ashore to meet with Him.

"Come and have breakfast," Jesus told them. None of the disciples dared ask Him, "Who are You?" because they knew it was the Lord.   Jesus came, took the bread, and gave it to them. He did the same with the fish. This was now the third time Jesus appeared to the disciples after He was raised from the dead. **John 21:12-14 (HCSB)**

Dead people do not eat; neither do their spirits or ghosts. Yet, here was the man, Jesus of Nazareth, on two separate occasions breaking bread and eating with the apostles. Why?   This was to tell them clearly that He had done what He promised and what the prophets had promised.   There is victory over death and the grave.   This Jesus, who clearly died on the cross at Calvary, has risen, and is very much alive.

You too can dine with Jesus.

Listen! I stand at the door and knock. If anyone hears My voice and opens the door, I will come in to him and have dinner with him, and he with Me.
Revelation 3:20 (HCSB)

He lives.   He lives.   Christ Jesus lives today.

74   KILLING GIANTS

DID YOU KNOW?

David gained fame because he killed the giant, Goliath. Scripture tells us that Goliath was ten feet tall, and carried a spear that was like a weaver's beam.   Yet David stood up to this man who was twice his own height and several times his weight.   David didn't fear because he knew that the battle was not his own, but would be won by God.   In the end, of course, David was victorious and Goliath was dead.

But did you know that Goliath was only one of several giants that confronted the Israelites?   There were three other giants who were killed by David's warriors in later wars with the Philistines.   They were Sippai, a child of Goliath, and Lahmi, a brother of Goliath, and another man who was so big that he had six fingers on each hand and six toes on each foot.

Here is the account of the battles from 1 Chronicles.

After this, a war broke out with the Philistines at Gezer. At that time Sibbecai the Hushathite killed Sippai, a descendant of the giants, and the Philistines were subdued.   Once again there was a battle with the Philistines, and Elhanan son of Jair killed Lahmi the brother of Goliath the Gittite. The shaft of his spear was like a weaver's beam.   There was still another battle at Gath where there was a man of extraordinary stature with six fingers [on each hand] and six toes [on each foot]—24 in all. He, too, was descended from the giant. When he taunted Israel, Jonathan son of David's brother Shimei killed him. 1 **Chronicles 20:4-7 (HCSB)**

God protected His people, the Israelites, from these giants. Just as He guided the stone from David's sling, He also guided the destruction of these additional frightening warriors. This same great God loves you just as much as He loved David. He will take down the giants who are threatening you, just as He did for David and his men. We need only to remember that the battles we face are not ours to fight, but are already won by the Lord. We need only to let Him do the fighting for us.

Who is fighting your giants? The only weapon you need is the Sword of the Lord.

75   FILLING THE TEMPLE

DID YOU KNOW?

King Solomon honored the Lord by preparing a feast of dedication for the Temple.   He brought the Ark of the Covenant to the Temple at Jerusalem.   There was a special place in the Temple that was reserved for the Ark of the Covenant.   Inside the Temple was a room that was called The Holy Place, but beyond that was a separate room called The Holy of Holies.   The Holy of Holies is the room reserved for the Ark.

The Ark represented the Lord.   It contained the Ten Commandments which were placed there by Moses. Nothing else was in the Ark.

> *Nothing was in the ark except the two stone tablets that Moses had put there at Horeb, where the LORD made a covenant with the Israelites when they came out of the land of Egypt.* ***1 Kings 8:9 (HCSB)***

But something special occurred when the priests came out of The Holy Place.   God moved in.

> *When the priests came out of the holy place, the cloud filled the LORD's temple, and because of the cloud, the priests were not able to continue*

*ministering, for the glory of the LORD filled the temple. **1 Kings 8:10-11 (HCSB)***

How wonderful it would be if the Lord would fill our houses of worship in such a manner.   There are some church sanctuaries where you can feel the very presence of the Lord, but there are some that are cold and empty.

But God does not live in a church building.   God cannot be contained in a man-made structure.   God lives in His Temple, but the Temple He occupies is the heart of man. And like the church buildings, there are those where the Lord is evident, and there are those that are cold and empty.

*Don't you know that your body is a sanctuary of the Holy Spirit who is in you, whom you have from God? You are not your own,   **1 Corinthians 6:19 (HCSB)***

How wonderful it would be if the Lord would fill our Temples (hearts) in such a manner… and He will ….   Just ask. Dedicate your temple (heart) to worshiping the Lord and He will fill you … His Temple …with His Holy Spirit.

76   ADAM'S ATONEMENT

DID YOU KNOW?

God seldom creates a punishment for those who disobey him; He is more likely to let us stew in the juices of our own making.   He has done this from the very beginning.

When Adam and Eve sinned in the Garden of Eden, they knew they had sinned; God didn't have to tell them.   As a matter of fact, they tried to hide from God, knowing that God was aware of their sin.

> *Then the man and his wife heard the sound of the LORD God walking in the garden at the time of the evening breeze, and they hid themselves from the LORD God among the trees of the garden.* **Genesis 3:8 (HCSB)**

There are two people you cannot hide from: God and yourself.   No matter where you go, both will be present because God is omnipresent (meaning He is everywhere at once).

But God said something strange at this point:

> *So the LORD God called out to the man and said to him, "Where are you?"* **Genesis 3:9 (HCSB)**

Does anyone suppose that God, who knows ALL things, really didn't know where Adam was?   Of course He knew.

Maybe He was asking Adam … Look at where you are as a result of what you have done.

> *And he (Adam) said, "I heard You in the garden and I was afraid because I was naked, so I hid." Then He asked, "Who told you that you were naked? Did you eat from the tree that I commanded you not to eat from?"* **Genesis 3:10-11 (HCSB)**

Notice that God let Adam condemn himself. God did not accuse … Satan is our accuser. Rather than accusing, God went into the repairing mode. Where Adam had covered himself with fig leaves, God gave him animal skins to cover his skin and his sin.

From the beginning of time, from the very first sin, God has shown that sin cannot be atoned for except by the shedding of blood. The animals had to die to cover Adam's nakedness.

Don't blame God if your actions bring you grief. You have brought the grief upon yourself. But there is no need to stew in those juices. You need to go to God and ask Him to cover your sin with His atonement. The blood that will cover you will not be the blood of an animal, as it was with Adam; it will be the blood of Jesus Christ.

77   LOOSENING A BOLT

DID YOU KNOW?

God likes us to rely on Him for everything.   When I was a brand new Christian, I never thought of asking God for simple things.   Through a dear mentor-brother named Bill, I learned how deep that relationship can and should be.

I began working on changing the thermostat of my car engine one day at about 8 AM.   Just remove two bolts at the very top of the Subaru engine, lift the cap, pull out the old thermostat, and replace everything in reverse of that order. But after the first bolt, everything came to an abrupt stop. For the next seven-plus hours I wrestled with the other bolt.

At about 4 PM, Bill walked into my garage and asked me what I was doing.   I told him I was trying to remove this ^(^)$)_*# bolt. (I told you I was a new Christian!)   Then he asked me what I thought was a dumb question: "Did you pray over it?"

"No, Bill, I didn't pray over it.   I don't think God cares much about bolts!"

"Who made it?" Bill asked …. And I said something like "Someone from Nagasaki trying to get even."

So Bill asked if I would mind if he prayed about it.   I said, "Sure, if you want to pray, go ahead and pray."   I knew it wouldn't do any good because I'd been at this bolt for almost 8 hours.

Bill asked if I would join him.   I said ok.   And then he wanted me to kneel down right there in my garage! Kneel on a garage floor! "Rather odd," I was thinking.   I went along with him and heard him say, 'Lord, Keith needs a lesson in faith.   He thinks you don't care about little things.   Will you loosen that bolt and ease his frustration please."

Then Bill stood and asked me for a wrench, which I gladly gave him so I could watch him learn his lesson on stuck bolts … but the lesson was mine when the bolt came out as if it were in butter.

> *You did not choose Me, but I chose you. I appointed you that you should go out and produce fruit and that your fruit should remain, so that whatever you ask the Father in My name, He will give you.* **John 15:16 (HCSB)**

Maybe your need is great; maybe it is small; maybe it is an everyday common need, or maybe a friend needs a liver transplant.   But the Master of our needs is master over ALL needs.   All you need is faith and the faithfulness to ask in the Name of Jesus.

78 YOU ASK AMISS

DID YOU KNOW?

"Stop in the name of the law!" You have heard it. They use that line in movies and on TV. A man is running away from a crime scene and the pursuing police officer yells, "Stop in the name of the law!" But what does that mean? What is the NAME of the law? Is the word "law" a magic "abra-kadabra" that makes the person stop in their tracks? I would think that if the person is a fleeing criminal, he wants to get away from the law rather than stop because someone has yelled "law" at them. What the officer means is for the suspect to stop because the officer commands it within "the authority" of the law.

With all that being said, we hear from our Lord and Savior an incredible promise.

> *Whatever you ask in My name, I will do it so that the Father may be glorified in the Son. If you ask Me anything in My name, I will do it.* ***John 14:13-14 (HCSB)***

Some think that this means you can ask for anything so long as you include the statement "in Jesus' Name" before you say "amen." With that magic statement you can get a new car, a million dollars from the lottery, a new spouse, or maybe even that elusive pot of gold.   Please don't believe this false doctrine of "name it and claim it."

Whatever you ask for "in the authority" of Jesus, it will be granted.   If God has called you to ask for it to fulfill what He has called you to do, ask; it is in the authority of God.   But Janis Joplin's concept in the song of "Lord, won't you buy me a color TV," is probably not in the authority of the Lord, and cannot therefore be claimed "in the name" of the Lord.

Jesus was teaching about ministry calling when He gave this instruction.   No scripture should be taken out of context. Here is what He said:

> *"I assure you: The one who believes in Me will also do the works that I do. And he will do even greater works than these, because I am going to the Father. Whatever you ask in My name, I will do it so that the Father may be glorified in the Son. If you ask Me anything in My name, I will do it.* **John 14:12-14 (HCSB)**
>
> *You ask and don't receive because you ask with wrong motives, so that you may spend it on your evil desires.* **James 4:3 (HCSB)**

79   CRUCIFY HIM!

DID YOU KNOW?

Everybody loves a hero.   When a presidential candidate wins a couple primary elections everybody seems to jump on the bandwagon and cheer him on to victory.   When a sports team gets on a roll of winning, they get a lot more viewers rooting for them.   Donors line up to give money to the college team that wins a championship. The school's sports programs and academic scholarship funds grow explosively.

Does anybody remember Buster Douglas?   Most people remember Mike Tyson.   He was the heavyweight champion of the boxing world.   He was a machine when he stepped into the ring.   Nobody stood a chance against Tyson.   But in 1990, a "nobody" named Buster Douglas knocked out the undefeatable Tyson in the tenth round.   Suddenly Buster was the new hero.   Tyson was the new loser.

A few months later, Buster fought against Evander Holyfield and was knocked out in the third round.   Buster went from hero to loser in one fight.

People are fickle.   They love the winner and have contempt for the loser.   They did the same thing to Jesus.   They cheered Him as He rode into Jerusalem on Palm Sunday.

Now He came near the path down the Mount of Olives, and the whole crowd of the disciples began to praise God joyfully with a loud voice for all the miracles they had seen: The King who comes in the name of the Lord is the blessed One. Peace in heaven and glory in the highest heaven! **Luke 19:37-38 (HCSB)**

Only four days later a crowd stood in a plaza, looking at a beaten and bloodied Jesus, and yelled, "Crucify him!"

Pilate asked them again, "Then what do you want me to do with the One you call the King of the Jews?" Again they shouted, "Crucify Him!" Then Pilate said to them, "Why? What has He done wrong?" But they shouted, "Crucify Him!" all the more. **Mark 15:12-14 (HCSB)**

Is your Lord susceptible to a popularity contest? Do we proclaim Him when everyone cheers, but deny Him when the mood of the crowd changes? How strong is your faith? How true is your faithfulness?

80 BABYLONIAN GOLD

DID YOU KNOW?

God punished Jerusalem severely, but promised to restore them at a later time.   All the gold and silver of the temple was taken away to Babylon with the Lord's permission. However, God promised that they would be returned in His time.

> *For this is what the LORD of Hosts says about the pillars, the sea, the water carts, and the rest of the articles that still remain in this city,   those Nebuchadnezzar king of Babylon did not take when he deported Jeconiah son of Jehoiakim, king of Judah, from Jerusalem to Babylon along with all the nobles of Judah and Jerusalem.   Yes, this is what the LORD of Hosts, the God of Israel, says about the articles that remain in the temple of the LORD, in the palace of the king of Judah, and in Jerusalem: 'They will be brought to Babylon and will remain there until I attend to them again.' [This is] the LORD's declaration. 'Then I will bring them up and restore them to this place.'" **Jeremiah 27:19-22 (HCSB)**

After seventy years, the time frame that God had set at the beginning of the Babylonian invasion, God restored the gold and silver to Jerusalem, and paid to rebuild the fallen temple and city.   He used the Babylonian King to make His promise come true.

This is what the King of Babylon ordered:

> *You are also to bring the silver and gold the king and his counselors have willingly given to the God of Israel, whose dwelling is in Jerusalem, and all the silver and gold you receive throughout the province of Babylon, together with the freewill offerings given by the people and the priests to the house of their God in Jerusalem. Then you are to buy with this money as many bulls, rams, and lambs as needed, along with their grain and drink offerings, and offer them on the altar at the house of your God in Jerusalem. You may do whatever seems best to you and your brothers with the rest of the silver and gold, according to the will of your God. You must deliver to the God of Jerusalem all the articles given to you for the service of the house of your God. You may use the royal treasury to pay for anything else needed for the house of your God.* **Ezra 7:15-20 (HCSB)**

God will keep all His promises to you just as truly. He has promised that if you will believe in Jesus and accept Him as your Lord and Savior, you will live with Him eternally. He promised to return to us in the clouds, just as He arose from us.

Do you believe these promises? God has NEVER broken a promise to His people. He will keep these as well. Have you given your faith to Jesus? Come to Him and watch His promises become a reality.

Amazing Grace
By Keith Rothra

Everyone should know Amazing Grace,

She lives down by the track.

She feeds the poor and broken there,

Despite her twisted back.

No one knows where she gets the food;

She's homeless just like they.

But there she comes, rain or shine,

To feed them every day.

She takes the ragged hem of her skirt

To wash their feet and face,

And prays salvation for this poor soul.

This is Amazing Grace.

"And the King will answer them, 'I assure you: Whatever you did for one of the least of these brothers of Mine, you did for Me.' **Matthew 25:40 (HCSB)**

81   FRUIT EVERY MONTH

DID YOU KNOW?

In heaven, there will never be night.   God will be the light because His glory will shine always through the Lamb, who is Jesus.   We read this in the Book of Revelation

> *"Each day its gates will never close because it will never be night there."* ***Revelation 21:25 (HCSB)***

However, it was pointed out to me another promise: we will have fruit provided for us for eternity.   It will grow from the trees on either side of the river of living water.

> *Then he showed me the river of living water, sparkling like crystal, flowing from the throne of God and of the Lamb down the middle of the broad street /of the city/. The tree of life was on both sides of the river, bearing 12 kinds of fruit, producing its fruit every month.* ***Revelation 22:1-3 (HCSB)***

However …. Yes, another however…. Another posing question was asked of me.   This one was posed to me at about three o'clock in the morning.   My dear wife woke me to ask this one: If new fruit will be provided every month, but there is no night, then how long is a month?

The simple answer that I shared with her at that one-eye-opened hour was this.   God is our provider.   He will never leave His people in that Holy City to starve.   There will be an everlasting new growth of provision for God's people in that great city of the New Jerusalem.

Since time ceases to exist in heaven, to read a month to mean approximately 30 days would make no sense. Understanding that time is man's invention and that to the Lord, a thousand years is but a day, God is not limited by such a ticking clock.   These trees will provide fruit for His people forever … ongoing without end.

> …. And remember, I am with you always, to the end of the age."   **Matthew 28:20 (HCSB)**

82   THE TRINITY

DID YOU KNOW?

The term "trinity" does not appear anywhere in the Bible, but every mainstream Christian denomination accepts the Trinity as a Biblical concept.   The Bible tells us that there is only one God.   Does that mean that the majority of Christendom is living in heresy against the Bible?   Not at all.

The Bible indicates the existence of God the Father, usually referring to Him simply as God… sometimes in all capitals GOD.   The Bible also refers to Jesus as the Son of God, but also calls Him God.   And there are verses that clearly refer to the Spirit of God in the term of Holy Spirit.   Does the Bible say that there are three gods?   No.   The Bible tell us that the three are one and the same God, but each unique.

When Jesus was baptized in the Jordan, we see the existence of God in the form of the Holy Spirit of God, and we hear the voice of God the Father speaking of Jesus.

> *After Jesus was baptized, He went up immediately from the water. The heavens suddenly opened for Him, and He saw the Spirit of God descending like a dove and coming down on Him.   And there came a voice from heaven: This is My beloved Son. I take delight in Him!*   ***Matthew 3:16-17 (HCSB)***

But the Bible tells us that Jesus was with God at the beginning of creation. John writes about Jesus as being with God, but that He also actually is God.

> *In the beginning was the Word, and the Word was with God, and the Word was God. He was with God in the beginning.* **John 1:1-2 (HCSB)**

At that beginning, described in the first verses in the Bible, we find that the creator God, in the person of Jesus, was accompanied by His Holy Spirit as the creation occurred.

> *In the beginning God created the heavens and the earth. Now the earth was formless and empty, darkness covered the surface of the watery depths, and the Spirit of God was hovering over the surface of the waters.* **Genesis 1:1-2 (HCSB)**

So, who or what is the Trinity? It is God, who is manifested in the person of God the Father, God the Son, and God the Holy Spirit. These three aspects of God appear throughout the Bible, sometimes all at one place, sometimes by two, sometimes individually. But they are all the same God. They are all the one and triune God.

83   SCARY STUFF

DID YOU KNOW?

Some people are afraid of the gospel.   Just hearing from God is downright frightening to them.   When you try to present the truth of God's mercy and grace to these people, they will shrink away, or even RUN away.   I know, because I was one of them for more than half of my life.

When a college friend tried to share his newfound salvation with me, I called him a Jesus freak and chased him away. He came back and invited me to hear him preach his first sermon.   In sympathy for him I attended the church service (a rarity for me at that time).   When the Holy Spirit was all over me at the close of the service, and Jimmy asked me to accept salvation, I was scared …. Yes, scared.   I left that church nearly running.

When the first gospel message was given, it scared the first people to hear it.

> *In the same region, shepherds were staying out in the fields and keeping watch at night over their flock. Then an angel of the Lord stood before them, and the glory of the Lord shone around them, and they were terrified.* **Luke 2:8-9 (HCSB)**

So it seems I wasn't the first person to be terrified by the messenger of God's love.   Mine tried to calm me, but I was too panicked, so I ran away.   The shepherds heard the softer words of the angelic host:

> *But the angel said to them, "Don't be afraid, for look, I proclaim to you good news of great joy that will be for all the people:* **Luke 2:10 (HCSB)**

Here is the message that was given to them:

> *Today a Savior, who is Messiah the Lord, was born for you in the city of David.* **Luke 2:11 (HCSB)**

If you promise to not throw this down and run away, let me give you a frightening message:

> *Today a Savior, who is Messiah the Lord, was born for you in the city of David.* **Luke 2:11 (HCSB)**

If you are still reading, you have passed the first test… you are not frightened away.   Now, can you share it with your friends without chasing them off?

84   OUT OF EGYPT
… AND OTHER PROPHECIES

DID YOU KNOW?

There were many prophecies about a coming Messiah.   There were several men who claimed to be Him; even today we hear of such men.   Christians believe that Jesus, of Galilee, is that man. But how do we know that this is the One?

Let's look at only a few of the predictions of the Messiah.

> *Bethlehem Ephrathah, you are small among the clans of Judah; One will come from you to be ruler over Israel for Me. His origin is from antiquity, from eternity.* **Micah 5:2 (HCSB)**

> *And Joseph also went up from the town of Nazareth in Galilee, to Judea, to the city of David, which is called Bethlehem, because he was of the house and family line of David, to be registered along with Mary, who was engaged to him and was pregnant. While they were there, the time came for her to give birth. Then she gave birth to her firstborn Son, and she wrapped Him snugly in cloth and laid Him in a feeding trough—because there was no room for them at the lodging place.* **Luke 2:4-7 (HCSB)**

> *After they were gone, an angel of the Lord suddenly appeared to Joseph in a dream, saying, "Get up! Take the child and His mother, flee to Egypt, and stay there until I*

tell you. For Herod is about to search for the child to destroy Him." **Matthew 2:13 (HCSB)**

So he got up, took the child and His mother during the night, and escaped to Egypt. He stayed there until Herod's death, so that what was spoken by the Lord through the prophet might be fulfilled: Out of Egypt I called My Son. **Matthew 2:14-15 (HCSB)**

All of these, and many more prophecies, were fulfilled by Jesus of Nazareth. Does that make Him the One? Lets look at the math.

How many children were born in Bethlehem? Many.

How many of those were of the line of David? Some.

How many of those some were from Nazareth? Probably one, but let's say there was more than one for the sake of argument.

How many of those precious few were taken to Egypt after their birth? Probably one.

And how many of those, if more than one, were born under a star to announce the event?

I think we have narrowed the field to one, and this is only a handful for more than 300 prophecies fulfilled by Jesus of Nazareth. Beyond a doubt, He is the Anointed One ... Emmanuel ... God with us.

85 THE AGE OF MAN

DID YOU KNOW?

God looked upon the world and saw such corruption among mankind that He decided to destroy all life with a great flood. He did allow one man, Noah, and his wife, his three sons, and their wives to survive this flood by being in an ark when the waters burst forth that brought the flood.

Adam, the first man, lived to be 930 years old.   Following the bloodline from Adam to Noah we discover some amazing facts.

Noah was born approximately 100 years after the death of Adam.   Adam missed the flood by about 700 years.

> *"In the six hundredth year of Noah's life, in the second month, on the seventeenth day of the month, on that day all the sources of the watery depths burst open, the floodgates of the sky were opened, and the rain fell on the earth 40 days and 40 nights."* **Genesis 7:11-12 (HCSB)**

Bear in mind that many people in those times lived over 700 years; the youngest recorded death before the flood was Lamech at 777 years. The oldest was Methuselah who attained 969 years before death.   His father, Enoch, walked with God, and at the youthful age of 365 was taken by God.

"Enoch walked with God; then he was not there because God took him." **Genesis 5:24 (HCSB)**

If we use the Bible's ages and times, the Great Flood occurred a little more than 1700 years after the creation of Adam.

After the flood, the age of man drastically fell, although Moses was about 80 when he began the forty-year desert trek.

"Moses was a hundred and twenty years old when he died…" **Deuteronomy 34:7 (HCSB)**

By the time of David, it had reduced to the current average age.

"Our lives last seventy years or, if we are strong, eighty years." **Psalm 90:10 (HCSB)**

So how long will you live? We really don't have that answer. God shared that through Jesus' brother James.

You don't even know what tomorrow will bring—what your life will be! For you are [like] smoke that appears for a little while, then vanishes. **James 4:14 (HCSB)**

The length of your life was determined by God long before you were created.

Your eyes saw me when I was formless; all [my] days were written in Your book and planned before a single one of them began. **Psalm 139:16 (HCSB)**

Let us spend our time … whatever that time may be … bringing fruit into God's Kingdom.   Then we will spend eternity with Him in His mansion.

86   ADVISING GOD

DID YOU KNOW?

Most people will agree that we need to serve God; but far too many of them want to serve Him in an advisory capacity. How many times have you heard someone criticize the Lord for the way their prayers have been (or have not been) answered.   How many times have you asked God why He was doing what He was doing?

We all do this from time to time, but is it the right attitude to portray toward the creator of the universe and all that is in it? When Job finally ran out of patience and asked God why this was happening to him, God had some pretty harsh words for Job.

> *Where were you when I established the earth? Tell [Me], if you have understanding. Who fixed its dimensions? Certainly you know! Who stretched a measuring line across it? What supports its foundations? Or who laid its cornerstone while the morning stars sang together and all the sons of God shouted for joy?* **Job 38:4-7 (HCSB)**

Sometimes it is hard to understand what God is doing. After all, He is God … with the mind of God … and we are mere creations with a mind that is incapable of comprehending even the existence of this God.   And so we ask Him why … and we question His unquestionable judgment.

Oh, the depth of the riches both of the wisdom and the knowledge of God! How unsearchable His judgments and untraceable His ways! For who has known the mind of the Lord? Or who has been His counselor? Or who has ever first given to Him, and has to be repaid? For from Him and through Him and to Him are all things. To Him be the glory forever. Amen. **Romans 11:33-36 (HCSB)**

It comes down to a little thing called faith.   Do we have enough faith to truly TRUST His judgment?

87   MARVIN'S PAPER WADS

DID YOU KNOW?

You have probably met him, or at least someone like him.
He was crazy.   That's what everyone said.   Marvin would
sit in study hall wadding up sheets of paper and stuffing
them under his leg at his desk.   And he would wait for Mrs.
Marston to walk by … and she always did … and as soon
as she had passed his desk he would nail her right in the
back of the head with a paper wad.   Then the drama
began.

"Marvin!   What are you doing?"   And Marvin would have
this look of total astonishment … horror … grief … and he
would say with such deep regret, "I'm sooooooorrry."   So
Mrs. Marston would say something like, "Don't you EVER do
anything like that again!"   And he would say, with his chin
against his chest, "OK.   I'm sorry."

And Mrs. Marston would turn around and take about two
steps and BAM!   He did it again.   And we heard the
same skit played out again.   "I'm soooooorrry!"   And I
actually believe that he was.   I believe that he just could
not contain himself.   The back of her head just BEGGED to
be nailed with a paper wad, and it was Marvin's job to take
care of it.

204

How many days did this happen? .... Several.   How many times in one class period ... about three.   Why did Mrs. Marston walk down that row?   I don't know, but it became almost a comedy.   Who was crazy, him or her?   How many times did she forgive Marvin? .... Every time.

> *For I do not understand what I am doing, because I do not practice what I want to do, but I do what I hate. … For I know that nothing good lives in me, that is, in my flesh. For the desire to do what is good is with me, but there is no ability to do it.* **Romans 7:15, 18 (HCSB)**

Paul said he did things that he knew were wrong when he was doing them ... but he still did them ... hating himself while he was doing it.   I think Paul had a lot in common with Marvin; I think Paul had a lot in common with me. How about you?

I sure am glad that God forgives.   Aren't you?

88 CHANGING DIRECTIONS

DID YOU KNOW?

When a drug addict gets away from their drugging habits, their old "friends" have trouble dealing with it.   When an alcoholic quits drinking, the same thing happens.   Friends come around and try to lure them back into their former ways.

I had a friend who changed overnight from a wild drinking, fighting, drugging carouser into a man of God who was bound for seminary to become a minister.   I called him to invite him to a party and he wouldn't come because people would be drinking.   I told him he had turned into a Jesus freak.   He thanked me.   I thought he was crazy.   None of his old friends wanted anything more to do with him.

I was being what Jeremiah said about Israel.

> *Each one betrays his friend; no one tells the truth. They have taught their tongues to speak lies; they wear themselves out doing wrong.   You live in /a world/ of deception. In /their/ deception they refuse to know Me. /This is/ the LORD's declaration.* ***Jeremiah 9:5-6 (HCSB)***

When a sinner turns from their old ways and comes to Jesus, the world rebels against them. I did this to my friend, and he tried to tell me about his newfound faith. It was thirteen years later before I found that same faith, and then my old "friends" told me that I was pursuing myths. Now I was the Jesus freak, and I thanked them for the label.

Paul writes of these people in Romans:

> *And because they did not think it worthwhile to acknowledge God, God delivered them over to a worthless mind to do what is morally wrong. They are filled with all unrighteousness, evil, greed, and wickedness. They are full of envy, murder, quarrels, deceit, and malice. They are gossips, slanderers, God-haters, arrogant, proud, boastful, inventors of evil, disobedient to parents, undiscerning, untrustworthy, unloving, and unmerciful. Although they know full well God's just sentence—that those who practice such things deserve to die—they not only do them, but even applaud others who practice them.* **Romans 1:28-32 (HCSB)**

If you are trapped in a dangerous world and you do not know how to escape … there is a way. Stop listening to those false friends, and find new ones in a church family of God. They will encourage your escape, and God will deliver you from your past. I have seen it in others … I have lived it personally. You too can be free of the snare that holds you. Ask Jesus.

89   REVENGE UPON AMALEK

DID YOU KNOW?

God keeps His promises.   Sometimes that is good news and sometimes that is bad news.   God promised you salvation if you will only accept His grace given through the blood shed by Jesus. You can rest assured that you can claim that eternity by fulfilling what God said to do … accept His Son Jesus.

There is the other side of that equation as well.   When God makes a promise to destroy, it will also be fulfilled.   God told the King of Israel, Saul, to go to the Amalekites and destroy them.   Kill the men, woman, children, infants, cows, horses and anything else that breathes.   If it breathes, make it stop.   You can read that story in 1 Samuel 15.

But why would a loving, caring, compassionate God want to do such a thing?   He did it because He was fulfilling His oath found in Exodus 17.

> *At Rephidim, Amalek came and fought against Israel.*
> ***Exodus 17:8 (HCSB)***
>
> *So Joshua defeated Amalek and his army with the sword.* ***Exodus 17:13 (HCSB)***

The descendants of Amalek, the Amalekites, attacked Israel when they were on their way to the promised land; even before the Israelites were sentenced to 40 years of wandering in the desert,. God promised that He would make these people pay for their vicious, unwarranted attack.

> *The LORD then said to Moses, "Write this down on a scroll as a reminder and recite it to Joshua: I will completely blot out the memory of Amalek under heaven."* **Exodus 17:14 (HCSB)**

Therefore, God kept His oath by sending Saul to kill them after the Israelites had settled in the Promised Land.

In this same sense, there are those who ask how a loving, caring, compassionate God could send anyone to Hell. The answer is the same: God will keep His promises. Those who are His people, He will protect. Those who oppose Him and His people, He will condemn.

God did not make Hell for you or for any human being. It was made for Satan and his supporters who rebelled against God and His people. God made Heaven for those who were His own. He will bring His own into Heaven; He will send those who rebel against Him to Hell. Why? Because He is a just God who keeps His promises.

Here is the simple challenge: Which eternity do you want? You can have Heaven or Hell. It is your choice; but remember that God keeps His end of the bargain. Now ... you choose.

90 THE GALILEE PROMISE

DID YOU KNOW?

When Jesus rose from the grave, He sent a special message to His apostles that only they would understand. Before dawn on the first day of the week, Mary Magdalene and another Mary went to the tomb of Jesus to finish His burial preparations.   When they got there, they were astonished because the stone covering the opening of the burial cave had been moved, and the body of their Lord was not where they expected to find it.

> But the angel told the women, "Don't be afraid, because I know you are looking for Jesus who was crucified. He is not here! For He has been resurrected, just as He said. Come and see the place where He lay. Then go quickly and tell His disciples, 'He has been raised from the dead. In fact, He is going ahead of you to Galilee; you will see Him there.' Listen, I have told you." *Matthew 28:5-7 (HCSB)*

This was a secret code of sorts.   It was something that would prove to the apostles that it truly was the resurrected Jesus that the ladies encountered.   What was the message?   He told them that He was going ahead of them into Galilee.   Then He added this: "Listen, I told you."

Three nights earlier Jesus shared the Passover meal with the apostles.   After Judas left to betray Jesus, the Lord told

210

them what he was about to do.   He would die, then resurrect Himself, and then precede the apostles into Galilee.

Did you get that?   He would precede them into Galilee. And then He told the ladies to tell the apostles that He was preceding them into Galilee, and added, "Listen, I told you."

> But after I have been resurrected, I will go ahead of you to Galilee." **Matthew 26:32 (HCSB)**

Oddly enough, Jesus would see most of them that night in the upper room, and again in the same location a week later. However, everything that Jesus says, He will do.

About forty days later, Jesus met with His apostles.   Can you guess where?   Here is what it says.

> The eleven disciples traveled to Galilee, to the mountain where Jesus had directed them. **Matthew 28:16 (HCSB)**

The Great Commission was given by Jesus to the apostles just before He ascended into heaven.   Where did that happen?   On a mountain top in Galilee.   The apostles knew that Jesus would be there because He told them before He died, and reminded them after He arose.

He has told us that He is coming back again "in the clouds." He will keep that promise just like the one about Galilee. Are you looking up?

91   Habakkuk's Prayer

DID YOU KNOW?

Did you ever have one of those weeks where everything breaks or goes wrong?

When the riding lawn mower hits a root and bends the main shaft into uselessness, and the push mower dies an ignominious death of oily smoke and noise of throwing a rod;

All this occurs right before the weed-eater comes apart in your hands;

When your regular car breaks down (two bolts holding the flywheel on are now bouncing around down there), and you borrow another car from a used-car lot to drive to work;

Then you back the borrowed car into your broken car;

When right after you bought a new car with the extra money you were going to have your boss tells you that you didn't get the promotion you knew you would get.

I was "blessed with all these things and more within one week.   There comes a time when it occurs to you to sit down and ask, "OK, Lord, what are you trying to tell me?"

Yes, all those things …. And God is still in charge and taking care of you.

Consider it a great joy, my brothers, whenever you experience various trials, knowing that the testing of *your faith produces endurance. But endurance must do its complete work, so that you may be mature and complete, lacking nothing. **James 1:2-4 (HCSB)***

There comes a time when faithful prayer is the most powerful gift God can provide. An unbreakable faith is what carries us through broken lawn equipment, but also failed crops, failed relationships, failed business opportunities, or unfulfilled expectations.

Habakkuk prayed such a prayer that is worth noting the next time you think the world has fallen off its axis.

> *Though the fig tree does not bud and there is no fruit on the vines, though the olive crop fails and the fields produce no food, though there are no sheep in the pen and no cattle in the stalls, yet I will triumph in Yahweh; I will rejoice in the God of my salvation!* **Habakkuk 3:17-18 (HCSB)**

35737358R00121

Made in the USA
San Bernardino, CA
02 July 2016